THE NATURE OF THE
JUDICIAL PROCESS

THE STORRS LECTURES DELIVERED AT
YALE UNIVERSITY

THE NATURE OF THE
JUDICIAL PROCESS

BY

BENJAMIN N. CARDOZO, LL.D.

NEW HAVEN AND LONDON
YALE UNIVERSITY PRESS

ISBN: 0–300–00346–3 (cloth)
     0–300–00033–2 (paper)

Printed in the United States of America by
BookCrafters, Inc., Fredericksburg, Virginia.

56   55   54   53   52   51   50

Contents

THE NATURE OF THE JUDICIAL PROCESS

Lecture I. Introduction. The Method of Philosophy.

THE work of deciding cases goes on every day in hundreds of courts throughout the land. Any judge, one might suppose, would find it easy to describe the process which he had followed a thousand times and more. Nothing could be farther from the truth. Let some intelligent layman ask him to explain: he will not go very far before taking refuge in the excuse that the language of craftsmen is unintelligible to those untutored in the craft. Such an excuse may cover with a semblance of respectability an otherwise ignominious retreat. It will hardly serve to still the pricks of curiosity and conscience. In moments of introspection, when there is no longer a necessity of putting off with a show of wisdom the uninitiated interlocutor, the troublesome problem will recur, and press for a solution. What is it that I do when I decide a case? To what sources of information do I appeal for guidance? In what proportions do I permit them to contribute to the result? In what proportions ought they to contribute? If a precedent is applicable, when do I refuse to follow it? If no precedent is applicable, how do I reach the rule that will make a precedent for the future? If I am seeking logical consistency, the symmetry of the legal structure, how far shall I seek it? At what point shall the quest be halted by some discrepant custom, by some consideration of the social welfare, by my own or the common standards of justice and morals? Into that strange compound which is brewed daily in the caldron of the courts, all these ingredients enter in varying proportions. I am not concerned to inquire whether judges ought to be allowed to brew such a compound at all. I take judge-made law as one of the existing realities of life. There, before us, is the brew. Not a judge on the bench but has had a hand in the making. The elements have not come together by chance. *Some* principle. however unavowed and inarticulate and subconscious, has regulated the infusion. It may not have been the same principle for all judges at any time, nor the same principle for any judge at all times. But a choice there has been, not a submission to the decree of Fate; and the considerations and motives determining the choice, even if often obscure, do not utterly resist analysis. In such attempt at analysis as I shall make, there will be need to distinguish between the conscious and the subconscious. I do not mean that even those considerations and motives which I shall class under the first head are always in consciousness distinctly, so that they will be recognized and named at sight. Not infrequently they hover near the surface. They may, however, with comparative readiness be isolated and tagged, and when thus labeled are quickly acknowledged as guiding principles of conduct. More subtle are the forces so far beneath the surface that they cannot reasonably be classified as other than subconscious. It is often through these subconscious forces that judges are kept consistent with themselves, and inconsistent with one another. We are reminded by William James in a telling page of his lectures on Pragmatism that every one of us has in truth an underlying philosophy of life, even those of us to whom the names and the notions of philosophy are unknown or anathema. There is in each of us a stream of tendency, whether you choose to call it philosophy or not,[1] which gives coherence and direction to thought and action. Judges cannot escape that current any more than other mortals. All their lives, forces which they do not recognize and cannot name, have been tugging at them—inherited instincts, traditional beliefs, acquired convictions; and the resultant is an outlook on life, a conception of social needs, a sense in James's phrase of "the total push and pressure of the cosmos," which, when reasons are nicely balanced, must determine where choice shall fall.

[1] Cf. N. M. Butler, "Philosophy," pp. 18, 43.

In this mental background every problem finds its setting. We may try to see things as objectively as we please. None the less, we can never see them with any eyes except our own. To that test they are all brought—a form of pleading or an act of parliament, the wrongs of paupers or the rights of princes, a village ordinance or a nation's charter.

I have little hope that I shall be able to state the formula which will rationalize this process for myself, much less for others. We must apply to the study of judge-made law that method of quantitative analysis which Mr. Wallas has applied with such fine results to the study of politics.[2] A richer scholarship than mine is requisite to do the work aright. But until that scholarship is found and enlists itself in the task, there may be a passing interest in an attempt to uncover the nature of the process by one who is himself an active agent, day by day, in keeping the process alive. That must be my apology for these introspective searchings of the spirit.

[2] "Human Nature in Politics," p. 138.

INTRODUCTION

Before we can determine the proportions of a blend, we must know the ingredients to be blended. Our first inquiry should therefore be: Where does the judge find the law which he embodies in his judgment? There are times when the source is obvious. The rule that fits the case may be supplied by the constitution or by statute. If that is so, the judge looks no farther. The correspondence ascertained, his duty is to obey. The constitution overrides a statute, but a statute, if consistent with the constitution, overrides the law of judges. In this sense, judge-made law is secondary and subordinate to the law that is made by legislators. It is true that codes and statutes do not render the judge superfluous, nor his work perfunctory and mechanical. There are gaps to be filled. There are doubts and ambiguities to be cleared. There are hardships and wrongs to be mitigated if not avoided. Interpretation is often spoken of as if it were nothing but the search and the discovery of a meaning which, however obscure and latent, had none the less a real and ascertainable pre-existence in the legislator's mind. The process is, indeed, that at times, but it is often something more. The ascertainment of intention may be the least of a judge's troubles in ascribing meaning to a statute. "The fact is," says Gray in his lectures on the "Nature and Sources of the Law,"[3] "that the difficulties of so-called interpretation arise when the legislature has had no meaning at all; when the question which is raised on the statute never occurred to it; when what the judges have to do is, not to determine what the legislature did mean on a point which was present to its mind, but to guess what it would have intended on a point not present to its mind, if the point had been present."[4] So Brütt:[5] "One weighty task of the system of the application of law consists then in this, to make more profound the discovery of the latent meaning of positive law. Much more important, however, is the second task which the system serves, namely

[3] Sec. 370, p. 165.

[4] Cf. Pound, "Courts and Legislation," 9 Modern Legal Philosophy Series, p. 226.

[5] "Die Kunst der Rechtsanwendung," p. 72.

the filling of the gaps which are found in every positive law in greater or less measure." You may call this process legislation, if you will. In any event, no system of *jus scriptum* has been able to escape the need of it. Today a great school of continental jurists is pleading for a still wider freedom of adaptation and construction. The statute, they say, is often fragmentary and ill-considered and unjust. The judge as the interpreter for the community of its sense of law and order must supply omissions, correct uncertainties, and harmonize results with justice through a method of free decision—"libre recherche scientifique." That is the view of Gény and Ehrlich and Gmelin and others.[6] Courts are to "search for light among the social elements of every kind that are the living force behind the facts they deal with."[7] The power thus put in their hands is great, and subject, like all power, to abuse; but we are not to flinch from granting it. In the long run "there is no guaranty of

[6] "Science of Legal Method," 9 Modern Legal Philosophy Series, pp. 4, 45, 65, 72, 124, 130, 159.

[7] Gény, "Méthode d'Interprétation et Sources en droit

justice," says Ehrlich,[8] "except the personality of the judge."[9] The same problems of method, the same contrasts between the letter and the spirit, are living problems in our own land and law. Above all in the field of constitutional law, the method of free decision has become, I think, the dominant one today The great generalities of the constitution have a content and a significance that vary from age to age. The method of free decision sees through the transitory particulars and reaches what is permanent behind them. Interpretation, thus enlarged, becomes more than the ascertainment of the meaning and intent of lawmakers whose collective will has been declared. It supplements the declaration, and fills the vacant spaces, by the same processes and methods that have built up the customary law. Codes and other statutes may

privé positif," vol. II, p. 180, sec. 176, ed. 1919; transl. o Modern Legal Philosophy Series, p. 45.

[8] P. 65, *supra;* "Freie Rechtsfindung und freie Rechtswissenschaft," 9 Modern Legal Philosophy Series.

[9] Cf. Gnaeus Flavius (Kantorowicz), "Der Kampf um Rechtswissenschaft," p. 48: "Von der Kultur des Richters hängt im letzten Grunde aller Fortschritt der Rechtsentwicklung ab."

threaten the judicial function with repression and disuse and atrophy. The function flourishes and persists by virtue of the human need to which it steadfastly responds. Justinian's prohibition of any commentary on the product of his codifiers is remembered only for its futility.[10]

I will dwell no further for the moment upon the significance of constitution and statute as sources of the law. The work of a judge in interpreting and developing them has indeed its problems and its difficulties, but they are problems and difficulties not different in kind or measure from those besetting him in other fields. I think they can be better studied when those fields have been explored. Sometimes the rule of constitution or of statute is clear, and then the difficulties vanish. Even when they are present, they lack at times some of that element of mystery which accompanies creative energy. We reach the land of mystery when constitution and statute are silent, and the judge must look to

[10] Gray, "Nature and Sources of the Law," sec. 395; Muirhead, "Roman Law," pp. 399, 400.

the common law for the rule that fits the case. He is the "living oracle of the law" in Blackstone's vivid phrase. Looking at Sir Oracle in action, viewing his work in the dry light of realism, how does he set about his task?

The first thing he does is to compare the case before him with the precedents, whether stored in his mind or hidden in the books. I do not mean that precedents are ultimate sources of the law, supplying the sole equipment that is needed for the legal armory, the sole tools, to borrow Maitland's phrase,[11] "in the legal smithy." Back of precedents are the basic juridical conceptions which are the postulates of judicial reasoning, and farther back are the habits of life, the institutions of society, in which those conceptions had their origin, and which, by a process of interaction, they have modified in turn.[12] None the less, in a system so highly developed as our

[11] Introduction to Gierke's "Political Theories of the Middle Age," p. viii.

[12] Saleilles, "De la Personnalité Juridique," p. 45; Ehrlich, "Grundlegung der Soziologie des Rechts," pp. 34, 35; Pound, "Proceedings of American Bar Assn. 1919," p. 455.

own, precedents have so covered the ground that they fix the point of departure from which the labor of the judge begins. Almost invariably, his first step is to examine and compare them. If they are plain and to the point, there may be need of nothing more. *Stare decisis* is at least the everyday working rule of our law. I shall have something to say later about the propriety of relaxing the rule in exceptional conditions. But unless those conditions are present, the work of deciding cases in accordance with precedents that plainly fit them is a process similar in its nature to that of deciding cases in accordance with a statute. It is a process of search, comparison, and little more. Some judges seldom get beyond that process in any case. Their notion of their duty is to match the colors of the case at hand against the colors of many sample cases spread out upon their desk. The sample nearest in shade supplies the applicable rule. But, of course, no system of living law can be evolved by such a process, and no judge of a high court, worthy of his office, views the function of his place so narrowly. If

that were all there was to our calling, there would
be little of intellectual interest about it. The man
who had the best card index of the cases would
also be the wisest judge. It is when the colors do
not match, when the references in the index fail,
when there is no decisive precedent, that the
serious business of the judge begins. He must
then fashion law for the litigants before him. In
fashioning it for them, he will be fashioning it for
others. The classic statement is Bacon's: "For
many times, the things deduced to judgment may
be meum and tuum, when the reason and consequence thereof may trench to point of estate."[13]
The sentence of today will make the right and
wrong of tomorrow. If the judge is to pronounce
it wisely, some principles of selection there must
be to guide him among all the potential judgments that compete for recognition.

In the life of the mind as in life elsewhere,
there is a tendency toward the reproduction of
kind. Every judgment has a generative power.
It begets in its own image. Every precedent, in

[13] "Essay on Judicature."

the words of Redlich, has a "directive force for future cases of the same or similar nature."[14] Until the sentence was pronounced, it was as yet in equilibrium. Its form and content were uncertain. Any one of many principles might lay hold of it and shape it. Once declared, it is a new stock of descent. It is charged with vital power. It is the source from which new principles or norms may spring to shape sentences thereafter. If we seek the psychological basis of this tendency, we shall find it, I suppose, in habit.[15] Whatever its psychological basis, it is one of the living forces of our law. Not all the progeny of principles begotten of a judgment survive, however, to maturity. Those that cannot prove their worth and strength by the test of experience are sacrificed mercilessly and thrown into the void. The common law does not work from pre-established truths of universal and inflexible validity to conclusions derived from them

[14] Redlich, "The Case Method in American Law Schools," Bulletin No. 8, Carnegie Foundation, p. 37.

[15] McDougall, "Social Psychology," p. 354; J. C. Gray, "Judicial Precedents," 9 Harvard L. R. 27.

deductively. Its method is inductive, and it draws its generalizations from particulars. The process has been admirably stated by Munroe Smith: "In their effort to give to the social sense of justice articulate expression in rules and in principles, the method of the lawfinding experts has always been experimental. The rules and principles of case law have never been treated as final truths, but as working hypotheses, continually retested in those great laboratories of the law, the courts of justice. Every new case is an experiment; and if the accepted rule which seems applicable yields a result which is felt to be unjust, the rule is reconsidered. It may not be modified at once, for the attempt to do absolute justice in every single case would make the development and maintenance of general rules impossible; but if a rule continues to work injustice, it will eventually be reformulated. The principles themselves are continually retested; for if the rules derived from a principle do not work well, the principle itself must ultimately be re-examined."[16]

[16] Munroe Smith, "Jurisprudence," Columbia Uni-

INTRODUCTION

The way in which this process of retesting and reformulating works may be followed in an example. Fifty years ago, I think it would have been stated as a general principle that A. may conduct his business as he pleases, even though the purpose is to cause loss to B., unless the act involves the creation of a nuisance.[17] Spite fences were the stock illustration, and the exemption from liability in such circumstances was supposed to illustrate not the exception, but the rule.[18] Such a rule may have been an adequate working principle to regulate the relations between individuals or classes in a simple or homogeneous community. With the growing complexity of social relations, its inadequacy was revealed. As particular controversies multiplied and the attempt was made to test them by the

versity Press, 1909, p. 21; cf. Pound, "Courts and Legislation," 7 Am. Pol. Science Rev. 361; 9 Modern Legal Philosophy Series, p. 214; Pollock, "Essays in Jurisprudence and Ethics," p. 246.

[17] Cooley, "Torts," 1st ed., p. 93; Pollock, "Torts," 10th ed., p. 21.

[18] Phelps v. Nowlen, 72 N. Y. 39; Rideout v. Knox, 148 Mass. 368.

old principle, it was found that there was something wrong in the results, and this led to a reformulation of the principle itself. Today, most judges are inclined to say that what was once thought to be the exception is the rule, and what was the rule is the exception. A. may never do anything in his business for the purpose of injuring another without reasonable and just excuse.[19] There has been a new generalization which, applied to new particulars, yields results more in harmony with past particulars, and, what is still more important, more consistent with the social welfare. This work of modification is gradual. It goes on inch by inch. Its effects must be measured by decades and even centuries. Thus measured, they are seen to have behind them the power and the pressure of the moving glacier.

We are not likely to underrate the force that has been exerted if we look back upon its work. "There is not a creed which is not shaken, not an accredited dogma which is not shown to be

[19] Lamb v. Cheney, 227 N. Y. 418; Aikens v. Wisconsin, 195 U. S. 194, 204; Pollock, "Torts," *supra*.

questionable, not a received tradition which does not threaten to dissolve."[20] Those are the words of a critic of life and letters writing forty years ago, and watching the growing scepticism of his day. I am tempted to apply his words to the history of the law. Hardly a rule of today but may be matched by its opposite of yesterday. Absolute liability for one's acts is today the exception; there must commonly be some tinge of fault, whether willful or negligent. Time was, however, when absolute liability was the rule.[21] Occasional reversions to the earlier type may be found in recent legislation.[22] Mutual promises give rise to an obligation, and their breach to a right of action for damages. Time was when the

[20] Arnold, "Essays in Criticism," second series, p. 1.

[21] Holdsworth, "History of English Law," 2, p. 41; Wigmore, "Responsibility for Tortious Acts," 7 Harvard L. R. 315, 383, 441; 3 Anglo-Am. Legal Essays 474; Smith, "Liability for Damage to Land," 33 Harvard L. R. 551; Ames, "Law and Morals," 22 Harvard L. R. 97, 99; Isaacs, "Fault and Liability," 31 Harvard L. R. 954.

[22] Cf. Duguit, "Les Transformations générales du droit privé depuis le Code Napoléon," Continental Legal Hist. Series, vol. XI, pp. 125, 126, secs. 40, 42.

obligation and the remedy were unknown unless the promise was under seal.[23] Rights of action may be assigned, and the buyer prosecute them to judgment though he bought for purposes of suit. Time was when the assignment was impossible, and the maintenance of the suit a crime. It is no basis today for an action of deceit to show, without more, that there has been the breach of an executory promise; yet the breach of an executory promise came to have a remedy in our law because it was held to be a deceit.[24] These changes or most of them have been wrought by judges. The men who wrought them used the same tools as the judges of today. The changes, as they were made in this case or that, may not have seemed momentous in the making. The result, however, when the process was prolonged throughout the years, has been not merely to supplement or modify; it has been to revolu-

[23] Holdsworth, *supra*, 2, p. 72; Ames, "History of Parol Contracts prior to Assumpsit," 3 Anglo-Am. Legal Essays 304.

[24] Holdsworth, *supra*, 3, pp. 330, 336; Ames, "History of Assumpsit," 3 Anglo-Am. Legal Essays 275, 276.

tionize and transform. For every tendency, one seems to see a counter-tendency; for every rule its antinomy. Nothing is stable. Nothing absolute. All is fluid and changeable. There is an endless "becoming." We are back with Heraclitus. That, I mean, is the average or aggregate impression which the picture leaves upon the mind. Doubtless in the last three centuries, some lines, once wavering, have become rigid. We leave more to legislatures today, and less perhaps to judges.[25] Yet even now there is change from decade to decade. The glacier still moves.

In this perpetual flux, the problem which confronts the judge is in reality a twofold one: he must first extract from the precedents the underlying principle, the *ratio decidendi;* he must then determine the path or direction along which the principle is to move and develop, if it is not to wither and die.

The first branch of the problem is the one to which we are accustomed to address ourselves

[25] F. C. Montague in "A Sketch of Legal History," Maitland and Montague, p. 161.

more consciously than to the other. Cases do not
unfold their principles for the asking. They yield
up their kernel slowly and painfully. The instance cannot lead to a generalization till we
know it as it is. That in itself is no easy task.
For the thing adjudged comes to us oftentimes
swathed in obscuring dicta, which must be
stripped off and cast aside. Judges differ greatly
in their reverence for the illustrations and com-
ments and side-remarks of their predecessors, to
make no mention of their own. All agree that
there may be dissent when the opinion is filed.
Some would seem to hold that there must be none
a moment thereafter. Plenary inspiration has
then descended upon the work of the majority.
No one, of course, avows such a belief, and yet
sometimes there is an approach to it in conduct.
I own that it is a good deal of a mystery to me
how judges, of all persons in the world, should
put their faith in dicta. A brief experience on the
bench was enough to reveal to me all sorts of
cracks and crevices and loopholes in my own
opinions when picked up a few months after de-

livery, and reread with due contrition. The persuasion that one's own infallibility is a myth leads by easy stages and with somewhat greater satisfaction to a refusal to ascribe infallibility to others. But dicta are not always ticketed as such, and one does not recognize them always at a glance. There is the constant need, as every law student knows, to separate the accidental and the non-essential from the essential and inherent. Let us assume, however, that this task has been achieved, and that the precedent is known as it really is. Let us assume too that the principle, latent within it, has been skillfully extracted and accurately stated. Only half or less than half of the work has yet been done. The problem remains to fix the bounds and the tendencies of development and growth, to set the directive force in motion along the right path at the parting of the ways.

The directive force of a principle may be exerted along the line of logical progression; this I will call the rule of analogy or the method of philosophy; along the line of historical de-

velopment; this I will call the method of evolution; along the line of the customs of the community; this I will call the method of tradition;
along the lines of justice, morals and social welfare, the *mores* of the day; and this I will call
the method of sociology.

I have put first among the principles of selection to guide our choice of paths, the rule of
analogy or the method of philosophy. In putting
it first, I do not mean to rate it as most important. On the contrary, it is often sacrificed to
others. I have put it first because it has, I think,
a certain presumption in its favor. Given a mass
of particulars, a congeries of judgments on re-
lated topics, the principle that unifies and
rationalizes them has a tendency, and a legitimate
one, to project and extend itself to new cases
within the limits of its capacity to unify and
rationalize. It has the primacy that comes from
natural and orderly and logical succession.
Homage is due to it over every competing principle that is unable by appeal to history or
tradition or policy or justice to make out a

better right. All sorts of deflecting forces may appear to contest its sway and absorb its power. At least, it is the heir presumptive. A pretender to the title will have to fight his way.

Great judges have sometimes spoken as if the principle of philosophy, i.e., of logical development, meant little or nothing in our law. Probably none of them in conduct was ever true to such a faith. Lord Halsbury said in Quinn v. Leathem, 1901, A. C. 495, 506: "A case is only an authority for what it actually decides. I entirely deny that it can be quoted for a proposition that may seem to follow logically from it. Such a mode of reasoning assumes that the law is necessarily a logical code, whereas every lawyer must acknowledge that the law is not always logical at all."[26] All this may be true, but we must not press the truth too far. Logical consistency does not cease to be a good because it is not the supreme good. Holmes has told us

[26] Cf. Bailhache, J., in Belfast Ropewalk Co. v. Bushell, 1918, 1 K. B. 210, 213: "Unfortunately or fortunately, I am not sure which, our law is not a science."

in a sentence which is now classic that "the life of the law has not been logic; it has been experience."[27] But Holmes did not tell us that logic is to be ignored when experience is silent. I am not to mar the symmetry of the legal structure by the introduction of inconsistencies and irrelevancies and artificial exceptions unless for some sufficient reason, which will commonly be some consideration of history or custom or policy or justice. Lacking such a reason, I must be logical, just as I must be impartial, and upon like grounds. It will not do to decide the same question one way between one set of litigants and the opposite way between another. "If a group of cases involves the same point, the parties expect the same decision. It would be a gross injustice to decide alternate cases on opposite principles. If a case was decided against me yesterday when I was defendant, I shall look for the same judgment today if I am plaintiff. To decide differently would raise a feeling of resentment and wrong in my breast; it would be an

[27] "The Common Law," p. 1.

33

infringement, material and moral, of my rights."[28]
Everyone feels the force of this sentiment when
two cases are the same. Adherence to precedent
must then be the rule rather than the exception
if litigants are to have faith in the even-handed
administration of justice in the courts. A sentiment like in kind, though different in degree, is
at the root of the tendency of precedent to extend itself along the lines of logical development.[29] No doubt the sentiment is powerfully
reinforced by what is often nothing but an intellectual passion for *elegantia juris*, for symmetry of form and substance.[30] That is an ideal
which can never fail to exert some measure of
attraction upon the professional experts who
make up the lawyer class. To the Roman lawyers, it meant much, more than it has meant
to English lawyers or to ours, certainly more

[28] W. G. Miller, "The Data of Jurisprudence," p.
335; cf. Gray, "Nature and Sources of the Law," sec.
420; Salmond, "Jurisprudence," p. 170.

[29] Cf. Gény, "Méthode d'Interprétation et Sources
en droit privé positif," vol. II, p. 119.

[30] W. G. Miller, *supra*, p. 281; Bryce, "Studies in
History and Jurisprudence," vol. II, p. 629.

than it has meant to clients. "The client,"
says Miller in his "Data of Jurisprudence,"[31]
"cares little for a 'beautiful' case! He wishes
it settled somehow on the most favorable terms
he can obtain." Even that is not always true. But
as a system of case law develops, the sordid
controversies of litigants are the stuff out of
which great and shining truths will ultimately
be shaped. The accidental and the transitory will
yield the essential and the permanent. The judge
who moulds the law by the method of philosophy
may be satisfying an intellectual craving for
symmetry of form and substance. But he is doing
something more. He is keeping the law true in
its response to a deep-seated and imperious sentiment. Only experts perhaps may be able to gauge
the quality of his work and appraise its significance. But their judgment, the judgment of the
lawyer class, will spread to others, and tinge the
common consciousness and the common faith.
In default of other tests, the method of philosophy must remain the organon of the courts if

[31] P. 1.

chance and favor are to be excluded, and the affairs of men are to be governed with the serene and impartial uniformity which is of the essence of the idea of law.

You will say that there is an intolerable vagueness in all this. If the method of philosophy is to be employed in the absence of a better one, some test of comparative fitness should be furnished. I hope, before I have ended, to sketch, though only in the broadest outline, the fundamental considerations by which the choice of methods should be governed. In the nature of things they can never be catalogued with precision. Much must be left to that deftness in the use of tools which the practice of an art develops. A few hints, a few suggestions, the rest must be trusted to the feeling of the artist. But for the moment, I am satisfied to establish the method of philosophy as one organon among several, leaving the choice of one or the other to be talked of later. Very likely I have labored unduly to establish its title to a place so modest. Above all, in the Law School of Yale University, the title will not be challenged. I say that because in the work of a brilliant teacher of this school, the late Wesley Newcomb Hohfeld, I find impressive recognition of the importance of this method, when kept within due limits, and some of the happiest illustrations of its legitimate employment. His treatise on "Fundamental Conceptions Applied in Judicial Reasoning" is in reality a plea that fundamental conceptions be analyzed more clearly, and their philosophical implications, their logical conclusions, developed more consistently. I do not mean to represent him as holding to the view that logical conclusions must always follow the conceptions developed by analysis. "No one saw more clearly than he that while the analytical matter is an indispensable tool, it is not an all-sufficient one for the lawyer."[32] "He emphasized over and over again" that "analytical work merely paves the way for other branches of jurisprudence, and that without the aid of the latter, satisfactory solutions of

[32] Introduction to Hohfeld's Treatise by W. W. Cook.

37

legal problems cannot be reached."[33] We must know where logic and philosophy lead even though we may determine to abandon them for other guides. The times will be many when we can do no better than follow where they point.

Example, if not better than precept, may at least prove to be easier. We may get some sense of the class of questions to which a method is adapted when we have studied the class of questions to which it has been applied. Let me give some haphazard illustrations of conclusions adopted by our law through the development of legal conceptions to logical conclusions. A. agrees to sell a chattel to B. Before title passes, the chattel is destroyed. The loss falls on the seller who has sued at law for the price.[34] A. agrees to sell a house and lot. Before title passes, the house is destroyed. The seller sues in equity for specific performance. The loss falls upon the

[33] Professor Cook's Introduction.

[34] Higgins v. Murray, 73 N. Y. 252, 254; 2 Williston on Contracts, sec. 962; N. Y. Personal Prop. Law, sec. 103a.

THE METHOD OF PHILOSOPHY

buyer.[35] That is probably the prevailing view, though its wisdom has been sharply criticized.[36] These variant conclusions are not dictated by variant considerations of policy or justice. They are projections of a principle to its logical outcome, or the outcome supposed to be logical. Equity treats that as done which ought to be done. Contracts for the sale of land, unlike most contracts for the sale of chattels, are within the jurisdiction of equity. The vendee is in equity the owner from the beginning. Therefore, the burdens as well as the benefits of ownership shall be his. Let me take as another illustration of my meaning the cases which define the rights of assignees of choses in action. In the discussion of these cases, you will find much conflict of opinion about fundamental conceptions. Some tell us that the assignee has a legal ownership.[37] Others say that his right is purely equitable.[38]

---

[35] Paine v. Meller, 6 Ves. 349, 352; Sewell v. Underhill, 197 N. Y. 168; 2 Williston on Contracts, sec. 931.

[36] 2 Williston on Contracts, sec. 940.

[37] Cook, 29 Harvard L. R. 816, 836.

[38] Williston, 30 Harvard L. R. 97; 31 *ibid*. 822.

Given, however, the fundamental conception, all agree in deducing its consequences by methods in which the preponderating element is the method of philosophy. We may find kindred illustrations in the law of trusts and contracts and in many other fields. It would be wearisome to accumulate them.

The directive force of logic does not always exert itself, however, along a single and unobstructed path. One principle or precedent, pushed to the limit of its logic, may point to one conclusion; another principle or precedent, followed with like logic, may point with equal certainty to another. In this conflict, we must choose between the two paths, selecting one or other, or perhaps striking out upon a third, which will be the resultant of the two forces in combination, or will represent the mean between extremes. Let me take as an illustration of such conflict the famous case of Riggs v. Palmer, 115 N. Y. 506. That case decided that a legatee who had murdered his testator would not be permitted by a court of equity to enjoy the benefits of the will. Conflicting principles were there in competition for the mastery. One of them prevailed, and vanquished all the others. There was the principle of the binding force of a will disposing of the estate of a testator in conformity with law. That principle, pushed to the limit of its logic, seemed to uphold the title of the murderer. There was the principle that civil courts may not add to the pains and penalties of crimes. That, pushed to the limit of its logic, seemed again to uphold his title. But over against these was another principle, of greater generality, its roots deeply fastened in universal sentiments of justice, the principle that no man should profit from his own inequity or take advantage of his own wrong. The logic of this principle prevailed over the logic of the others. I say its logic prevailed. The thing which really interests us, however, is why and how the choice was made between one logic and another. In this instance, the reason is not obscure. One path was followed, another closed, because of the conviction in the judicial mind that the one selected led to justice. Analogies and precedents and the principles behind them were brought together as rivals for precedence; in the end, the principle that was thought to be most fundamental, to represent the larger and deeper social interests, put its competitors to flight. I am not greatly concerned about the particular formula through which justice was attained. Consistency was preserved, logic received its tribute, by holding that the legal title passed, but that it was subjected to a constructive trust.[39] A constructive trust is nothing but "the formula through which the conscience of equity finds expression."[40] Property is acquired in such circumstances that the holder of the legal title may not in good conscience retain the beneficial interest. Equity, to express its disapproval of his conduct, converts him into a trustee.[41] Such formulas are merely the remedial devices by which a result conceived of as right and just is

[39] Ellerson v. Westcott, 148 N. Y. 149, 154; Ames, "Lectures on Legal History," pp. 313, 314.

[40] Beatty v. Guggenheim Exploration Co., 225 N. Y. 380, 386.

[41] Beatty v. Guggenheim Exploration Co., *supra;* Ames, *supra.*

made to square with principle and with the symmetry of the legal system. What concerns me now is not the remedial device, but rather the underlying motive, the indwelling, creative energy, which brings such devices into play. The murderer lost the legacy for which the murder was committed because the social interest served by refusing to permit the criminal to profit by his crime is greater than that served by the preservation and enforcement of legal rights of ownership. My illustration, indeed, has brought me ahead of my story. The judicial process is there in microcosm. We go forward with our logic, with our analogies, with our philosophies, till we reach a certain point. At first, we have no trouble with the paths; they follow the same lines. Then they begin to diverge, and we must make a choice between them. History or custom or social utility or some compelling sentiment of justice or sometimes perhaps a semi-intuitive apprehension of the pervading spirit of our law must come to the rescue of the anxious judge, and tell him where to go.

It is easy to accumulate examples of the process—of the constant checking and testing of philosophy by justice, and of justice by philosophy. Take the rule which permits recovery with compensation for defects in cases of substantial, though incomplete performance. We have often applied it for the protection of builders who in trifling details and without evil purpose have departed from their contracts. The courts had some trouble for a time, when they were deciding such cases, to square their justice with their logic. Even now, an uneasy feeling betrays itself in treatise and decision that the two fabrics do not fit. As I had occasion to say in a recent case: "Those who think more of symmetry and logic in the development of legal rules than of practical adaptation to the attainment of a just result" remain "troubled by a classification where the lines of division are so wavering and blurred."[42] I have no doubt that the inspiration of the rule is a mere sentiment of justice. That sentiment asserting itself, we have proceeded to surround it

[42] Jacobs & Youngs, Inc. v. Kent, 230 N. Y. 239.

44

with the halo of conformity to precedent. Some judges saw the unifying principle in the law of quasi-contracts. Others saw it in the distinction between dependent and independent promises, or between promises and conditions. All found, however, in the end that there *was* a principle in the legal armory which, when taken down from the wall where it was rusting, was capable of furnishing a weapon for the fight and of hewing a path to justice. Justice reacted upon logic, sentiment upon reason, by guiding the choice to be made between one logic and another. Reason in its turn reacted upon sentiment by purging it of what is arbitrary, by checking it when it might otherwise have been extravagant, by relating it to method and order and coherence and tradition.[43]

In this conception of the method of logic or philosophy as one organon among several, I find nothing hostile to the teachings of continental jurists who would dethrone it from its place and

[43] Cf. Hynes v. N. Y. Central R. R. Co. (231 N. Y. 229, 235).

power in systems of jurisprudence other than our own. They have combated an evil which has touched the common law only here and there, and lightly. I do not mean that there are not fields where we have stood in need of the same lesson. In some part, however, we have been saved by the inductive process through which our case law has developed from evils and dangers inseparable from the development of law, upon the basis of the *jus scriptum*, by a process of deduction.[44] Yet even continental jurists who emphasize the need of other methods, do not ask us to abstract from legal principles all their fructifying power. The misuse of logic or philosophy begins when its method and its ends are treated as supreme and final. They can never be banished altogether. "Assuredly," says François Gény,[45] "there should be no question of banishing ratiocination and logical methods from the

[44] "Notre droit public, comme notre droit privé, est un *jus scriptum*" (Michoud, "La Responsibilité de l'état à raison des fautes de ses agents," Revue du droit public, 1895, p. 273, quoted by Gény, vol. I, p. 40, sec. 19).

[45] *Op. cit.*, vol. I, p. 127, sec. 61.

science of positive law." Even general principles may sometimes be followed rigorously in the deduction of their consequences. "The abuse," he says, "consists, if I do not mistake, in envisaging ideal conceptions, provisional and purely subjective in their nature, as endowed with a permanent objective reality. And this false point of view, which, to my thinking, is a vestige of the absolute realism of the middle ages, ends in confining the entire system of positive law, *a priori*, within a limited number of logical categories, which are predetermined in essence, immovable in basis, governed by inflexible dogmas, and thus incapable of adapting themselves to the ever varied and changing exigencies of life."

In law, as in every other branch of knowledge, the truths given by induction tend to form the premises for new deductions. The lawyers and the judges of successive generations do not repeat for themselves the process of verification, any more than most of us repeat the demonstrations of the truths of astronomy or physics. A stock of juridical conceptions and formulas is developed, and we take them, so to speak, ready-made. Such fundamental conceptions as contract and possession and ownership and testament and many others are there, ready for use. How they came to be there, I do not need to inquire. I am writing, not a history of the evolution of law, but a sketch of the judicial process applied to law full grown. These fundamental conceptions once attained form the starting point from which are derived new consequences, which, at first tentative and groping, gain by reiteration a new permanence and certainty. In the end, they become accepted themselves as fundamental and axiomatic. So it is with the growth from precedent to precedent. The implications of a decision may in the beginning be equivocal. New cases by commentary and exposition extract the essence. At last there emerges a rule or principle which becomes a datum, a point of departure, from which new lines will be run, from which new courses will be measured. Sometimes the rule or principle is found to have been formulated too narrowly or too broadly, and has to be reframed.

Sometimes it is accepted as a postulate of later reasoning, its origins are forgotten, it becomes a new stock of descent, its issue unite with other strains, and persisting permeate the law. You may call the process one of analogy or of logic or of philosophy as you please. Its essence in any event is the derivation of a consequence from a rule or a principle or a precedent which, accepted as a datum, contains implicitly within itself the germ of the conclusion. In all this, I do not use the word philosophy in any strict or formal sense. The method tapers down from the syllogism at one end to mere analogy at the other. Sometimes the extension of a precedent goes to the limit of its logic. Sometimes it does not go so far. Sometimes by a process of analogy it is carried even farther. That is a tool which no system of jurisprudence has been able to discard.[46] A rule which has worked well in one field, or which, in any event, is there whether its workings have been revealed or not, is carried over into another. Instances of such a process I group

[46] Ehrlich, "Die Juristische Logik," pp. 225, 227.

under the same heading as those where the nexus of logic is closer and more binding.[47] At bottom and in their underlying motives, they are phases of the same method. They are inspired by the same yearning for consistency, for certainty, for uniformity of plan and structure. They have their roots in the constant striving of the mind for a larger and more inclusive unity, in which differences will be reconciled, and abnormalities will vanish.

[47] Cf. Gény, *op. cit.*, vol. II, p. 121, sec. 165; also vol. I, p. 304, sec. 107.

Lecture II.   The Methods of History, Tradition and Sociology

THE method of philosophy comes in competition, however, with other tendencies which find their outlet in other methods. One of these is the historical method, or the method of evolution. The tendency of a principle to expand itself to the limit of its logic may be counteracted by the tendency to confine itself within the limits of its history. I do not mean that even then the two methods are always in opposition. A classification which treats them as distinct is, doubtless, subject to the reproach that it involves a certain overlapping of the lines and principles of division. Very often, the effect of history is to make the path of logic clear.[1] Growth may be logical whether it is shaped by the principle

[1] Cf. Holmes, "The Path of the Law," 10 Harvard L. R. 465.

of consistency with the past or by that of consistency with some pre-established norm, some general conception, some "indwelling, and creative principle."[2] The directive force of the precedent may be found either in the events that made it what it is, or in some principle which enables us to say of it that it is what it ought to be. Development may involve either an investigation of origins or an effort of pure reason. Both methods have their logic. For the moment, however, it will be convenient to identify the method of history with the one, and to confine the method of logic or philosophy to the other. Some conceptions of the law owe their existing form almost exclusively to history. They are not to be understood except as historical growths. In the development of such principles, history is likely to predominate over logic or pure reason. Other conceptions, though they have, of course, a history, have taken form and shape to a larger extent under the influence of reason or of com-

[2] Bryce, "Studies in History and Jurisprudence," vol. II, p. 609.

parative jurisprudence. They are part of the *jus gentium.* In the development of such principles logic is likely to predominate over history. An illustration is the conception of juristic or corporate personality with the long train of consequences which that conception has engendered. Sometimes the subject matter will lend itself as naturally to one method as to another. In such circumstances, considerations of custom or utility will often be present to regulate the choice. A residuum will be left where the personality of the judge, his taste, his training or his bent of mind, may prove the controlling factor. I do not mean that the directive force of history, even where its claims are most assertive, confines the law of the future to uninspired repetition of the law of the present and the past. I mean simply that history, in illuminating the past, illuminates the present, and in illuminating the present, illuminates the future. "If at one time it seemed likely," says Maitland,[3] "that the historical spirit (the spirit which strove to understand the classi-

[3] "Collected Papers," vol. III, p. 438.

cal jurisprudence of Rome and the Twelve Tables, and the Lex Salica, and law of all ages and climes) was fatalistic and inimical to reform, that time already lies in the past. . . . Nowadays we may see the office of historical research as that of explaining, and therefore lightening, the pressure that the past must exercise upon the present, and the present upon the future. Today we study the day before yesterday, in order that yesterday may not paralyze today, and today may not paralyze tomorrow."

Let me speak first of those fields where there can be no progress without history. I think the law of real property supplies the readiest example.[4] No lawgiver meditating a code of laws conceived the system of feudal tenures. History built up the system and the law that went with it. Never by a process of logical deduction from the idea of abstract ownership could we distinguish the incidents of an estate in fee simple from those of an estate for life, or those of an estate for life from those of an estate for years. Upon

[4] Techt v. Hughes, 229 N. Y. 222, 240.

these points, "a page of history is worth a volume of logic."[5] So it is wherever we turn in the forest of the law of land. Restraints upon alienation, the suspension of absolute ownership, contingent remainders, executory devises, private trusts and trusts for charities, all these heads of the law are intelligible only in the light of history, and get from history the impetus which must shape their subsequent development. I do not mean that even in this field the method of philosophy plays no part at all. Some of the conceptions of the land law, once fixed, are pushed to their logical conclusions with inexorable severity. The point is rather that the conceptions themselves have come to us from without and not from within, that they embody the thought, not so much of the present as of the past, that separated from the past their form and meaning are unintelligible and arbitrary, and hence that their development, in order to be truly logical, must be mindful of their origins. In a measure that is true of most of the

[5] Holmes, J., in N. Y. Trust Co. v. Eisner, 256 U. S. 345, 349.

55

conceptions of our law. Metaphysical principles have seldom been their life. If I emphasize the law of real estate, it is merely as a conspicuous example. Other illustrations, even though less conspicuous, abound. "The forms of action we have buried," says Maitland,[6] "but they still rule us from their graves." Holmes has the same thought:[7] "If we consider the law of contract," he says, "we find it full of history. The distinctions between debt, covenant and assumpsit are merely historical. The classification of certain obligations to pay money, imposed by the law irrespective of any bargain as quasi-contracts, is merely historical. The doctrine of consideration is merely historical. The effect given to a seal is to be explained by history alone." The powers and functions of an executor, the distinctions between larceny and embezzlement, the rules of venue and the jurisdiction over foreign trespass, these are a few haphazard illustrations of growths which history has fostered, and which history

[6] "Equity and Forms of Action," p. 296.
[7] "The Path of the Law," 10 Harvard L. R. 472.

56

must tend to shape. There are times when the
subject matter lends itself almost indifferently to
the application of one method or another, and the
predilection or training of the judge determines
the choice of paths. The subject has been pene-
tratingly discussed by Pound.[8] I borrow one of
his illustrations. Is a gift of movables *inter vivos*
effective without delivery? The controversy raged
for many years before it was set at rest. Some
judges relied on the analogy of the Roman Law.
Others upon the history of forms of conveyance
in our law. With some, it was the analysis of
fundamental conceptions, followed by the extension of the results of analysis to logical conclusions. The declared will to give and to accept
was to have that effect and no more which was
consistent with some pre-established definition
of a legal transaction, an act in the law. With
others, the central thought was not consistency
with a conception, the consideration of what
logically ought to be done, but rather consistency

[8] "Juristic Science and the Law," 31 Harvard L. R.
1047.

57

with history, the consideration of what had been done. I think the opinions in Lumley v. Gye, 2 El. & Bl. 216, which established a right of action against A. for malicious interference with a contract between B. and C., exhibit the same divergent strains, the same variance in emphasis. Often, the two methods supplement each other. Which method will predominate in any case may depend at times upon intuitions of convenience or fitness too subtle to be formulated, too imponderable to be valued, too volatile to be localized or even fully apprehended. Sometimes the prevailing tendencies exhibited in the current writings of philosophical jurists may sway the balance. There are vogues and fashions in jurisprudence as in literature and art and dress. But of this there will be more to say when we deal with the forces that work subconsciously in the shaping of the law.

If history and philosophy do not serve to fix the direction of a principle, custom may step in. When we speak of custom, we may mean more things than one. "Consuetudo," says Coke, "is one of the maine triangles of the lawes of England; these lawes being divided into common law, statute law and customs."[9] Here common law and custom are thought of as distinct. Not so, however, Blackstone: "This unwritten or Common Law is properly distinguishable into three kinds: (1) General customs, which are the universal rule of the whole Kingdom, and form the Common Law, in its stricter and more usual signification. (2) Particular customs, which for the most part affect only the inhabitants of particular districts. (3) Certain particular laws, which by custom are adopted and used by some particular courts of pretty general and extensive jurisdiction."[10]

Undoubtedly the creative energy of custom in the development of common law is less today than it was in bygone times.[11] Even in bygone

[9] Coke on Littleton, 62a; Post v. Pearsall, 22 Wend. 440.

[10] Blackstone, Comm., pp. 67, 68; Gray, "Nature and Sources of the Law," p. 266, sec. 598; Sadler, "The Relation of Custom to Law," p. 59.

[11] Cf. Gray, *supra*, sec. 634; Salmond, "Jurisprudence," p. 143; Gény, *op. cit.*, vol. I, p. 324, sec. 111.

times, its energy was very likely exaggerated by Blackstone and his followers. "Today we recognize," in the words of Pound,[12] "that the custom is a custom of judicial decision, not of popular action." It is "doubtful," says Gray,[13] "whether at all stages of legal history, rules laid down by judges have not generated custom, rather than custom generated the rules." In these days, at all events, we look to custom, not so much for the creation of new rules, but for the tests and standards that are to determine how established rules shall be applied. When custom seeks to do more than this, there is a growing tendency in the law to leave development to legislation. Judges do not feel the same need of putting the *imprimatur* of law upon customs of recent growth, knocking for entrance into the legal system, and viewed askance because of some novel aspect of form or feature, as they would if legislatures were not in frequent session, capable of establishing a title that will be unimpeached and unimpeach-

[12] "Common Law and Legislation," 21 Harvard L. R. 383, 406.
[13] *Supra,* sec. 634.

able. But the power is not lost because it is exercised with caution. "The law merchant," says an English judge, "is not fixed and stereotyped, it has not yet been arrested in its growth by being moulded into a code; it is, to use the words of Lord Chief Justice Cockburn in Goodwin v. Roberts, L. R. 10 Exch. 346, capable of being expanded and enlarged to meet the wants of trade."[14] In the absence of inconsistent statute, new classes of negotiable instruments may be created by mercantile practice.[15] The obligations of public and private corporations may retain the quality of negotiability, despite the presence of a seal, which at common law would destroy it. "There is nothing immoral or contrary to good policy in making them negotiable if the necessities of commerce require that they should be so. A mere technical dogma of the courts or the common law cannot prohibit the commercial world from inventing or issuing any species of

[14] Edelstein v. Schuler, 1902, 2 K. B. 144, 154; cf. Bechuanaland Exploration Co. v. London Trading Bank, 1898, 2 Q. B. 658.

[15] Cases, *supra*.

security not known in the last century."[16] So, in the memory of men yet living, the great inventions that embodied the power of steam and electricity, the railroad and the steamship, the telegraph and the telephone, have built up new customs and new law. Already there is a body of legal literature that deals with the legal problems of the air.

It is, however, not so much in the making of new rules as in the application of old ones that the creative energy of custom most often manifests itself today. General standards of right and duty are established. Custom must determine whether there has been adherence or departure. My partner has the powers that are usual in the trade. They may be so well known that the courts will notice them judicially. Such for illustration is the power of a member of a trading firm to make or indorse negotiable paper in the course of the firm's business.[17] They may be

[16] Mercer County v. Hacket, 1 Wall. 83; cf. Chase Nat. Bank v. Faurot, 149 N. Y. 532.
[17] Lewy v. Johnson, 2 Pet. 186.

such that the court will require evidence of
their existence.[18] The master in the discharge of
his duty to protect the servant against harm
must exercise the degree of care that is commonly
exercised in like circumstance by men of ordinary
prudence. The triers of the facts in determining
whether that standard has been attained must
consult the habits of life, the everyday beliefs
and practices, of the men and women about
them. Innumerable, also, are the cases where the
course of dealing to be followed is defined by the
customs, or, more properly speaking, the usages,
of a particular trade or market or profession.[19]
The constant assumption runs throughout the
law that the natural and spontaneous evolutions
of habit fix the limits of right and wrong. A slight
extension of custom identifies it with customary
morality, the prevailing standard of right conduct, the *mores* of the time.[20] This is the point

[18] First Nat. Bank v. Farson, 226 N. Y. 218.

[19] Irwin v. Williar, 110 U. S. 499, 513; Walls v.
Bailey, 49 N. Y. 464; 2 Williston on Contracts, sec.
649.

[20] Cf. Gény, *op. cit.*, vol. I, p. 319, sec. 110.

of contact between the method of tradition and the method of sociology. They have their roots in the same soil. Each method maintains the interaction between conduct and order, between life and law. Life casts the moulds of conduct, which will some day become fixed as law. Law preserves the moulds, which have taken form and shape from life.

Three of the directive forces of our law, philosophy, history and custom, have now been seen at work. We have gone far enough to appreciate the complexity of the problem. We see that to determine to be loyal to precedents and to the principles back of precedents does not carry us far upon the road. Principles are complex bundles. It is well enough to say that we shall be consistent, but consistent with what? Shall it be consistency with the origins of the rule, the course and tendency of development? Shall it be consistency with logic or philosophy or the fundamental conceptions of jurisprudence as disclosed by analysis of our own and foreign systems? All these loyalties are possible. All have

sometimes prevailed. How are we to choose between them? Putting that question aside, how do
we choose between them? Some concepts of the
law have been in a peculiar sense historical
growths. In such departments, history will tend
to give direction to development. In other departments, certain large and fundamental concepts,
which comparative jurisprudence shows to be
common to other highly developed systems, loom
up above all others. In these we shall give a
larger scope to logic and symmetry. A broad field
there also is in which rules may, with approxi-
mately the same convenience, be settled one way
or the other. Here custom tends to assert itself
as the controlling force in guiding the choice of
paths. Finally, when the social needs demand
one settlement rather than another, there are
times when we must bend symmetry, ignore history and sacrifice custom in the pursuit of other
and larger ends.

From history and philosophy and custom, we
pass, therefore, to the force which in our day
and generation is becoming the greatest of them

all, the power of social justice which finds its outlet and expression in the method of sociology.

The final cause of law is the welfare of society. The rule that misses its aim cannot permanently justify its existence. "Ethical considerations can no more be excluded from the administration of justice which is the end and purpose of all civil laws than one can exclude the vital air from his room and live."[21] Logic and history and custom have their place. We will shape the law to conform to them when we may; but only within bounds. The end which the law serves will dominate them all. There is an old legend that on one occasion God prayed, and his prayer was "Be it my will that my justice be ruled by my mercy." That is a prayer which we all need to utter at times when the demon of formalism tempts the intellect with the lure of scientific order. I do not mean, of course, that judges are commissioned to set aside existing rules at pleasure in favor of any other

[21] Dillon, "Laws and Jurisprudence of England and America," p. 18, quoted by Pound, 27 Harvard L. R. 731, 733.

set of rules which they may hold to be expedient or wise. I mean that when they are called upon to say how far existing rules are to be extended or restricted, they must let the welfare of society fix the path, its direction and its distance. We are not to forget, said Sir George Jessel, in an often quoted judgment, that there is this paramount public policy, that we are not lightly to interfere with freedom of contract.[22] So in this field, there may be a paramount public policy, one that will prevail over temporary inconvenience or occasional hardship, not lightly to sacrifice certainty and uniformity and order and coherence. All these elements must be considered. They are to be given such weight as sound judgment dictates. They are constituents of that social welfare which it is our business to discover.[23] In a given instance we may find that they are constituents of preponderating value. In others, we may find that their value is subordinate. We must appraise them as best we can.

[22] Printing etc. Registering Co. v. Sampson, L. R 19 Eq. 462, 465.
[23] Cf. Brütt, *supra*, pp. 161, 163.

I have said that judges are not commissioned to make and unmake rules at pleasure in accordance with changing views of expediency or wisdom. Our judges cannot say with Hobbes: "Princes succeed one another, and one judge passeth, another cometh; nay heaven and earth shall pass, but not one tittle of the law of nature shall pass, for it is the eternal law of God. Therefore, all the sentences of precedent judges that have ever been cannot altogether make a law contrary to natural equity, nor any examples of former judges can warrant an unreasonable sentence or discharge the present judge of the trouble of studying what is equity in the case he is to judge from the principles of his own natural reason."[24] Nearer to the truth for us are the words of an English judge: "Our common law system consists in applying to new combinations of circumstances those rules of law which we derive from legal principles and judicial precedents, and for the sake of attaining uniformity, con-

[24] Hobbes, vol. II, p. 264; quoted by W. G. Miller, "The Data of Jurisprudence," p. 399.

sistency and certainty, we must apply those rules
when they are not plainly unreasonable and in-
convenient to all cases which arise; and we are
not at liberty to reject them and to abandon all
analogy to them in those in which they have not
yet been judicially applied, because we think that
the rules are not as convenient and reasonable as
we ourselves could have devised."[25] This does not
mean that there are not gaps, yet unfilled, within
which judgment moves untrammeled. Mr. Justice Holmes has summed it up in one of his flash-
ing epigrams: "I recognize without hesitation
that judges must and do legislate, but they do so
only interstitially; they are confined from molar
to molecular motions. A common-law judge could
not say, I think the doctrine of consideration a
bit of historical nonsense and shall not enforce
it in my court."[26] This conception of the legislative power of a judge as operating between spaces
is akin to the theory of "gaps in the law" familiar

[25] Sir James Parke, afterward Lord Wensleydale,
in Mirehouse v. Russell, 1 Cl. & F. 527, 546, quoted by
Ehrlich, "Grundlegung der Soziologie des Rechts"
[1913], p. 234; cf. Pollock, "Jurisprudence," p. 323.

[26] Southern Pacific Co. v. Jensen, 244 U. S. 205, 221.

to foreign jurists.[27] "The general framework furnished by the statute is to be filled in for each case by means of interpretation, that is, by following out the principles of the statute. In every case, without exception, it is the business of the court to supply what the statute omits, but always by means of an interpretative function."[28] If the statute is interpreted by the method of "free decision," the process differs in degree rather than in kind from the process followed by the judges of England and America in the development of the common law. Indeed, Ehrlich in a recent book[29] quotes approvingly an English writer, who says[30] that "a code would not, except in a few cases, in which the law at present is obscure, limit any discretion now pos-

[27] 9 Modern Legal Philosophy Series, pp. 159–163, 172–175; cf. Ehrlich, "Die juristische Logik," pp. 215, 216; Zitelmann, "Lücken im Recht," p. 23; Brütt, "Die Kunst der Rechtsanwendung," p. 75; Stammler, "Die Lehre von dem richtigen Rechte," p. 271.

[28] Kiss, "Equity and Law," 9 Modern Legal Philosophy Series, p. 161.

[29] "Grundlegung der Soziologie des Rechts" [1913], p. 234.

[30] 19 L. Q. R. 15.

70

sessed by the judges. It would simply change the form of the rules by which they are bound." I think that statement overshoots the mark. The fissures in the common law are wider than the fissures in a statute, at least in the form of statute common in England and the United States. In countries where statutes are oftener confined to the announcement of general principles, and there is no attempt to deal with details or particulars, legislation has less tendency to limit the freedom of the judge. That is why in our own law there is often greater freedom of choice in the construction of constitutions than in that of ordinary statutes. Constitutions are more likely to enunciate general principles, which must be worked out and applied thereafter to particular conditions. What concerns us now, however, is not the size of the gaps. It is rather the principle that shall determine how they are to be filled, whether their size be great or small. The method of sociology in filling the gaps puts its emphasis on the social welfare.

Social welfare is a broad term. I use it to

71

cover many concepts more or less allied. It may mean what is commonly spoken of as public policy, the good of the collective body. In such cases, its demands are often those of mere expediency or prudence. It may mean on the other hand the social gain that is wrought by adherence to the standards of right conduct, which find expression in the *mores* of the community. In such cases, its demands are those of religion or of ethics or of the social sense of justice, whether formulated in creed or system, or immanent in the common mind. One does not readily find a single term to cover these and kindred aims which shade off into one another by imperceptible gradations. Perhaps we might fall back with Kohler[31] and Brütt[32] and Berolzheimer[33] on the indefinable, but comprehensive something known as Kultur, if recent history had not discredited it and threatened odium for

[31] Enzyklopadie, Bd. 1, D. 10; Philosophy of Law, 12 Modern Legal Philosophy Series, p. 58.

[32] *Supra*, p. 133, *et seq.*

[33] "System des Rechts und Wirthschaftsphilosophie," Bd. 3, s. 28.

those that use it. I have chosen in its stead a term which, if not precise enough for the philosopher, will at least be found sufficiently definite and inclusive to suit the purposes of the judge.

It is true, I think, today in every department of the law that the social value of a rule has become a test of growing power and importance. This truth is powerfully driven home to the lawyers of this country in the writings of Dean Pound. "Perhaps the most significant advance in the modern science of law is the change from the analytical to the functional attitude."[34] "The emphasis has changed from the content of the precept and the existence of the remedy to the effect of the precept in action and the availability and efficiency of the remedy to attain the ends for which the precept was devised."[35] Foreign jurists have the same thought: "The whole of the judicial function," says Gmelin,[36]

[34] Pound, "Administrative Application of Legal Standards," Proceedings American Bar Association, 1919, pp. 441, 449.

[35] *Ibid.*, p. 451; cf. Pound, "Mechanical Jurisprudence," 8 Columbia L. R. 603.

[36] "Sociological Method," transl., 9 Modern Legal Philosophy Series, p. 131.

"has . . . been shifted. The will of the State, expressed in decision and judgment is to bring about a just determination by means of the subjective sense of justice inherent in the judge, guided by an effective weighing of the interests of the parties in the light of the opinions generally prevailing among the community regarding transactions like those in question. The determination should under all circumstances be in harmony with the requirements of good faith in business intercourse and the needs of practical life, unless a positive statute prevents it; and in weighing conflicting interests, the interest that is better founded in reason and more worthy of protection should be helped to achieve victory."[37]

"On the one hand," says Gény,[38] "we are to interrogate reason and conscience, to discover in our inmost nature, the very basis of justice; on the other, we are to address ourselves to social

[37] Gmelin, *supra;* cf. Ehrlich, "Die juristische Logik," p. 187; Duguit, "Les Transformations du droit depuis le Code Napoléon," transl., Continental Legal Hist. Series, vol. XI, pp. 72, 70.

[38] *Op. cit.*, vol. II, p. 92, sec. 159.

phenomena, to ascertain the laws of their harmony and the principles of order which they exact." And again:[39] "Justice and general utility, such will be the two objectives that will direct our course."

All departments of the law have been touched and elevated by this spirit. In some, however, the method of sociology works in harmony with the method of philosophy or of evolution or of tradition. Those, therefore, are the fields where logic and coherence and consistency must still be sought as ends. In others, it seems to displace the methods that compete with it. Those are the fields where the virtues of consistency must yield within those interstitial limits where judicial power moves. In a sense it is true that we are applying the method of sociology when we pursue logic and coherence and consistency as the greater social values. I am concerned for the moment with the fields in which the method is in antagonism to others rather than with those in which their action is in unison. Accurate divi-

[39] Vol. II, p. 91.

sion is, of course, impossible. A few broad areas may, however, be roughly marked as those in which the method of sociology has fruitful application. Let me seek some illustrations of its workings. I will look for them first of all in the field of constitutional law, where the primacy of this method is, I think, undoubted, then in certain branches of private law where public policy, having created rules, must have like capacity to alter them, and finally in other fields where the method, though less insistent and pervasive, stands ever in the background, and emerges to the front when technicality or logic or tradition may seem to press their claims unduly.

I speak first of the constitution, and in particular of the great immunities with which it surrounds the individual. No one shall be deprived of liberty without due process of law. Here is a concept of the greatest generality. Yet it is put before the courts *en bloc*. Liberty is not defined. Its limits are not mapped and charted. How shall they be known? Does liberty mean the

76

same thing for successive generations? May restraints that were arbitrary yesterday be useful
and rational and therefore lawful today? May
restraints that are arbitrary today become useful and rational and therefore lawful tomorrow?
I have no doubt that the answer to these questions must be yes. There were times in our
judicial history when the answer might have been
no. Liberty was conceived of at first as something
static and absolute. The Declaration of Independence had enshrined it. The blood of Revolution had sanctified it. The political philosophy
of Rousseau and of Locke and later of Herbert
Spencer and of the Manchester school of economists had dignified and rationalized it. *Laissez
faire* was not only a counsel of caution which
statesmen would do well to heed. It was a categorical imperative which statesmen, as well as
judges, must obey. The "nineteenth century
theory" was "one of eternal legal conceptions involved in the very idea of justice and containing
potentially an exact rule for every case to be
reached by an absolute process of logical deduc-

77

tion."[40] The century had not closed, however, before a new political philosophy became reflected in the work of statesmen and ultimately in the decrees of courts. The transition is interestingly described by Dicey in his "Law and Opinion in England."[41] "The movement from individualistic liberalism to unsystematic collectivism" had brought changes in the social order which carried with them the need of a new formulation of fundamental rights and duties. In our country, the need did not assert itself so soon. Courts still spoke in the phrases of a philosophy that had served its day.[42] Gradually, however, though not without frequent protest and intermittent movements backward, a new conception of the significance of constitutional limitations in the domain of individual liberty, emerged to recognition and to dominance. Judge Hough, in an interesting address, finds the dawn

[40] Pound, "Juristic Science and the Law," 31 Harvard L. R. 1047, 1048.

[41] Cf. Duguit, *supra*.

[42] Haines, "The Law of Nature in Federal Decisions," 25 Yale L. J. 617.

of the new epoch in 1883, when Hurtado v. California, 110 U. S. 516, was argued.[43] If the new epoch had then dawned, it was still obscured by fog and cloud. Scattered rays of light may have heralded the coming day. They were not enough to blaze the path. Even as late as 1905, the decision in Lochner v. N. Y., 198 U. S. 45, still spoke in terms untouched by the light of the new spirit. It is the dissenting opinion of Justice Holmes, which men will turn to in the future as the beginning of an era.[44] In the instance, it was the voice of a minority. In principle, it has become the voice of a new dispensation, which has written itself into law. "The Fourteenth Amendment does not enact Mr. Herbert Spencer's Social Statics."[45] "A constitution is not intended to embody a particular economic theory, whether of paternalism and the organic relation of the citizen to the state, or of *laissez*

[43] Hough, "Due Process of Law Today," 32 Harvard L. R. 218, 227.

[44] Cf. Hough, p. 232; also Frankfurter, "Const. Opinions of Holmes, J.," 29 Harvard L. R. 683, 687; Ehrlich, "Die juristische Logik," pp. 237, 239.

[45] 198 U. S. 75.

79

faire.[46] "The word liberty in the Fourteenth Amendment is perverted when it is held to prevent the natural outcome of a dominant opinion, unless it can be said that a rational and fair man necessarily would admit that the statute proposed would infringe fundamental principles as they have been understood by the traditions of our people and our law."[47] That is the conception of liberty which is dominant today.[48] It has its critics even yet,[49] but its dominance is, I think, assured. No doubt, there will at times be difference of opinion when a conception so delicate is applied to varying conditions.[50] At times, indeed, the conditions themselves are imperfectly disclosed and inadequately known. Many and insidious are the agencies by which opinion is poisoned at its sources. Courts have often been

[46] P. 75.

[47] P. 76.

[48] Noble v. State Bank, 219 U. S. 104; Tanner v. Little, 240 U. S. 369; Hall v. Geiger Jones Co., 242 U. S. 539; Green v. Frazier, 253 U. S. 233; Frankfurter, *supra.*

[49] Burgess, "Reconciliation of Government and Liberty."

[50] Adams v. Tanner, 244 U. S. 590.

HISTORY, TRADITION AND SOCIOLOGY

led into error in passing upon the validity of a statute, not from misunderstanding of the law, but from misunderstanding of the facts. This happened in New York. A statute forbidding night work for women was declared arbitrary and void in 1907.[51] In 1915, with fuller knowledge of the investigations of social workers, a like statute was held to be reasonable and valid.[52] Courts know today that statutes are to be viewed, not in isolation or *in vacuo,* as pronouncements of abstract principles for the guidance of an ideal community, but in the setting and the framework of present-day conditions, as revealed by the labors of economists and students of the social sciences in our own country and abroad.[53] The same fluid and dynamic conception which underlies the modern notion of liberty, as secured to the individual by the constitutional immunity,

[51] People v. Williams, 189 N. Y. 131.

[52] People v. Schweinler Press, 214 N. Y. 395.

[53] Muller v. Oregon, 208 U. S. 412; Pound, "Courts and Legislation," 9 Modern Legal Philosophy Series, p. 225; Pound, "Scope and Progress of Sociological Jurisprudence," 25 Harvard L. R. 513; cf. Brandeis, J., in Adams v. Tanner, 244 U. S. 590, 600.

HISTORY, TRADITION AND SOCIOLOGY

must also underlie the cognate notion of equality.
No state shall deny to any person within its
jurisdiction "the equal protection of the laws."[54]
Restrictions, viewed narrowly, may seem to
foster inequality. The same restrictions, when
viewed broadly, may be seen "to be necessary
in the long run in order to establish the equality
of position between the parties in which liberty
of contract begins."[55] Charmont in "La Renaissance du droit naturel,"[56] gives neat expression
to the same thought: "On tend à considerer qu'il
n'y a pas de contrat respectable si les parties
n'ont pas été placées dans les conditions non
seulement de liberté, mais d'égalité. Si l'un des
contractants est sans abri, sans ressources, con-
damné à subir les exigences de l'autre, la liberté
de fait est supprimée."[57]

From all this, it results that the content of

[54] U. S. Const., 14th Amendment.

[55] Holmes, J., dissenting in Coppage v. Kansas, 236
U. S. 1, 27.

[56] Montpellier, Coulet et fils, éditeurs, 1910.

[57] "There is now a tendency to consider no contract
worthy of respect unless the parties to it are in relations, not only of liberty, but of equality. If one of the

constitutional immunities is not constant, but varies from age to age. "The needs of successive generations may make restrictions imperative today, which were vain and capricious to the vision of times past."[58] "We must never forget," in Marshall's mighty phrase, "that it is a *constitution* we are expounding."[59] Statutes are designed to meet the fugitive exigencies of the hour. Amendment is easy as the exigencies change. In such cases, the meaning, once construed, tends legitimately to stereotype itself in the form first cast. A *constitution* states or ought to state not rules for the passing hour, but principles for an expanding future. In so far as it deviates from that standard, and descends into details and particulars, it loses its flexibility, the scope of interpretation contracts, the meaning

parties be without defense or resources, compelled to comply with the demands of the other, the result is a suppression of true freedom."—Charmont, *supra*, p. 172; transl. in 7 Modern Legal Philosophy Series, p. 110. sec. 83.

[58] Klein v. Maravelas, 219 N. Y. 383, 386.

[59] Cf. Frankfurter, *supra;* McCulloch v. Maryland, 4 Wheat. 407.

hardens. While it is true to its function, it maintains its power of adaptation, its suppleness, its play. I think it is interesting to note that even in the interpretation of ordinary statutes, there are jurists, at any rate abroad, who maintain that the meaning of today is not always the meaning of tomorrow. "The President of the highest French Court, M. Ballot-Beaupré, explained, a few years ago, that the provisions of the Napoleonic legislation had been adapted to modern conditions by a judicial interpretation in *'le sens évolutif.'* 'We do not inquire,' he said, 'what the legislator willed a century ago, but what he would have willed if he had known what our present conditions would be.' "[60] So Kohler: "It follows from all this that the interpretation of a statute must by no means of necessity remain the same forever. To speak of an exclusively correct interpretation, one which would be the true meaning of the statute from the begin-

[60] Munroe Smith, "Jurisprudence," pp. 29, 30; cf. Vander Eycken, *supra,* pp. 383, 384; also Brütt, *supra,* p. 62.

ning to the end of its days, is altogether erroneous."[61] I think the instances must be rare, if any can be found at all, in which this method of interpretation has been applied in English or American law to ordinary legislation. I have no doubt that it has been applied in the past and with increasing frequency will be applied in the future, to fix the scope and meaning of the broad precepts and immunities in state and national constitutions. I see no reason why it may not be applied to statutes framed upon lines similarly general, if any such there are. We are to read them, whether the result be contraction or expansion, in *"le sens évolutif."*[62]

Apposite illustrations may be found in recent statutes and decisions. It was long ago held by the Supreme Court that the legislature had the power to control and regulate a business affected

[61] Kohler, "Interpretation of Law," transl. in 9 Modern Legal Philosophy Series, 192; cf. the Report of Prof. Huber on the German Code, quoted by Gény, "Technic of Codes," 9 Modern Legal Philosophy Series, p. 548; also Gény, "Méthode et Sources en droit privé positif," vol. I, p. 273.

[62] Munroe Smith, *supra*.

with "a public use."[63] It is held by the Supreme
Court today that there is a like power where the
business is affected with "a public interest."[64]
The business of fire insurance has been brought
within that category.[65] A recent decision of an
inferior court has put within the same category
the business of the sale of coal where the emer-
gency of war or of the dislocation that results
from war brings hardship and oppression in the
train of unfettered competition.[66] The advocates
of the recent housing statutes in New York[67] profess to find in like principles the justification for
new restraints upon ancient rights of property. I
do not suggest any opinion upon the question
whether those acts in any of their aspects may
be held to go too far. I do no more than indicate
the nature of the problem, and the method and
spirit of approach.[68]

[63] Munn v. Illinois, 94 U. S. 113.

[64] German Alliance Ins. Co. v. Kansas, 233 U. S. 389.

[65] German Alliance Ins. Co. v. Kansas, *supra*.

[66] American Coal Mining Co. v. Coal & Food Com-
mission, U. S. District Court, Indiana, Sept. 6, 1920.

[67] L. 1920, chaps. 942 to 953.

[68] Since these lectures were written, the statutes have
been sustained: People *ex rel.* Durham Realty Co. v.

Property, like liberty, though immune under the Constitution from destruction, is not immune from regulation essential for the common good. What that regulation shall be, every generation must work out for itself.[69] The generation which gave us Munn v. Illinois, 94 U. S. 113 (1876), and like cases, asserted the right of regulation whenever business was "affected with a public use." The phrase in its application meant little more than if it said whenever the social need shall be imminent and pressing. Such a formulation of the principle may have been adequate for the exigencies of the time. Today there is a growing tendency in political and juristic thought to probe the principle more deeply and formulate it more broadly. Men are saying today that property, like every other social institution, has a social function to fulfill. Legislation which destroys the institution is one thing. Legislation which holds it true to its function is quite another. That is the dominant theme of a new and

La Fetra, 230 N. Y. 429; Marcus Brown Holding Co. v. Feldman, 256 U. S. 170.

[69] Green v. Frazier, 253 U. S. 233.

forceful school of publicists and jurists on the continent of Europe, in England, and even here. Among the French, one may find the thought developed with great power and suggestiveness by Duguit in his "Transformations générales du droit privé depuis le Code Napoléon."[70] It is yet too early to say how far this new conception of function and its obligations will gain a lodgment in our law. Perhaps we shall find in the end that it is little more than Munn v. Illinois in the garb of a new philosophy. I do not attempt to predict the extent to which we shall adopt it, or even to assert that we shall adopt it at all. Enough for my purpose at present that new times and new manners may call for new standards and new rules.

The courts, then, are free in marking the limits of the individual's immunities to shape their judgments in accordance with reason and justice. That does not mean that in judging the validity of statutes they are free to substitute

[70] Transl., Continental Legal Hist. Series, vol. XI, p. 74, sec. 6, *et seq.;* for a more extreme view, see R. H. Tawney, "The Acquisitive Society."

their own ideas of reason and justice for those of the men and women whom they serve. Their standard must be an objective one. In such matters, the thing that counts is not what I believe to be right. It is what I may reasonably believe that some other man of normal intellect and conscience might reasonably look upon as right. "While the courts must exercise a judgment of their own, it by no means is true that every law is void which may seem to the judges who pass upon it excessive, unsuited to its ostensible end, or based upon conceptions of morality with which they disagree. Considerable latitude must be allowed for difference of view as well as for possible peculiar conditions which this court can know but imperfectly, if at all. Otherwise a constitution, instead of embodying only relatively fundamental rules of right, as generally understood by all English-speaking communities, would become the partisan of a particular set of ethical or economical opinions, which by no means are held *semper ubique et ab omnibus.*"[71]

[71] Otis v. Parker, 187 U. S. 608.

Here as so often in the law, "the standard of conduct is external, and takes no account of the personal equation of the man concerned."[72] "The interpreter," says Brütt,[73] "must above all things put aside his estimate of political and legislative values, and must endeavor to ascertain in a purely objective spirit what ordering of the social life of the community comports best with the aim of the law in question in the circumstances before him." Some fields of the law there are, indeed, where there is freer scope for subjective vision. Of these we shall say more hereafter. The personal element, whatever its scope in other spheres, should have little, if any, sway in determining the limits of legislative power. One department of the government may not force upon another its own standards of propriety. "It must be remembered that legislatures are ultimate guardians of the liberties and welfare of the people in quite as great a degree as courts."[74]

[72] The Germanic, 196 U. S. 589, 596.

[73] "Die Kunst der Rechtsanwendung," p. 57.

[74] Missouri, K. & T. Co. v. May, 194 U. S. 267, 270; People v. Crane, 214 N. Y. 154, 173.

Some critics of our public law insist that the power of the courts to fix the limits of permissible encroachment by statute upon the liberty of the individual is one that ought to be withdrawn.[75] It means, they say, either too much or too little. If it is freely exercised, if it is made an excuse for imposing the individual beliefs and philosophies of the judges upon other branches of the government, if it stereotypes legislation within the forms and limits that were expedient in the nineteenth or perhaps the eighteenth century, it shackles progress, and breeds distrust and suspicion of the courts. If, on the other hand, it is interpreted in the broad and variable sense which I believe to be the true one, if statutes are to be sustained unless they are so plainly arbitrary and oppressive that right-minded men and women could not reasonably regard them otherwise, the right of supervision, it is said, is not worth the danger of abuse. "There no doubt comes a time when a statute is so obviously oppressive and ab-

[75] Cf. Collins, "The 14th Amendment and the States," pp. 158, 166.

91

surd that it can have no justification in any sane polity."[76] Such times may indeed come, yet only seldom. The occasions must be few when legislatures will enact a statute that will merit condemnation upon the application of a test so liberal; and if carelessness or haste or momentary passion may at rare intervals bring such statutes into being with hardship to individuals or classes, we may trust to succeeding legislatures for the undoing of the wrong. That is the argument of the critics of the existing system. My own belief is that it lays too little stress on the value of the "imponderables." The utility of an external power restraining the legislative judgment is not to be measured by counting the occasions of its exercise. The great ideals of liberty and equality are preserved against the assaults of opportunism, the expediency of the passing hour, the erosion of small encroachments, the scorn and derision of those who have no patience with general principles, by enshrining them in constitutions, and

[76] Learned Hand, "Due Process of Law and the Eight Hour Day," 21 Harvard L. R. 495, 508.

consecrating to the task of their protection a body of defenders. By conscious or subconscious influence, the presence of this restraining power, aloof in the background, but none the less always in reserve, tends to stabilize and rationalize the legislative judgment, to infuse it with the glow of principle, to hold the standard aloft and visible for those who must run the race and keep the faith.[77] I do not mean to deny that there have been times when the possibility of judicial review has worked the other way. Legislatures have sometimes disregarded their own responsibility, and passed it on to the courts. Such dangers must be balanced against those of independence from all restraint, independence on the part of public officers elected for brief terms, without the guiding force of a continuous tradition. On the whole, I believe the latter dangers to be the more formidable of the two. Great maxims, if they may be violated with impunity, are honored often with lip-service, which passes

[77] Cf. Laski, "Authority in the Modern State," pp. 62, 63.

easily into irreverence. The restraining power of the judiciary does not manifest its chief worth in the few cases in which the legislature has gone beyond the lines that mark the limits of discretion. Rather shall we find its chief worth in making vocal and audible the ideals that might otherwise be silenced, in giving them continuity of life and of expression, in guiding and directing choice within the limits where choice ranges. This function should preserve to the courts the power that now belongs to them, if only the power is exercised with insight into social values, and with suppleness of adaptation to changing social needs.

I pass to another field where the dominance of the method of sociology may be reckoned as assured. There are some rules of private law which have been shaped in their creation by public policy, and this, not merely silently or in conjunction with other forces, but avowedly, and almost, if not quite, exclusively. These, public policy, as determined by new conditions, is competent to change. I take as an illustration modern decisions which have liberalized the common law rule condemning contracts in restraint of trade. The courts have here allowed themselves a freedom of action which in many branches of the law they might be reluctant to avow. Lord Watson put the matter bluntly in Nordenfeldt v. Maxim, Nordenfeldt Guns & Ammunition Co. L. R. 1894 App. Cas. 535, 553: "A series of decisions based upon grounds of public policy, however eminent the judges by whom they were delivered, cannot possess the same binding authority as decisions which deal with and formulate principles which are purely legal. The course of policy pursued by any country in relation to, and for promoting the interests of, its commerce must, as time advances and as its commerce thrives, undergo change and development from various causes which are altogether independent of the action of its courts. In England, at least, it is beyond the jurisdiction of her tribunals to mould and stereotype national policy. Their function, when a case like the present is brought before them, is, in my opinion, not necessarily to accept what was held to have been the rule of policy a hundred or a hundred and fifty years ago, but to ascertain, with as near an approach to accuracy as circumstances permit, what is the rule of policy for the then present time. When that rule has been ascertained, it becomes their duty to refuse to give effect to a private contract which violates the rule, and would, if judicially enforced, prove injurious to the community." A like thought finds expression in the opinions of our own courts. "Arbitrary rules which were originally well founded have thus been made to yield to changed conditions, and underlying principles are applied to existing methods of doing business. The tendencies in most of the American courts are in the same direction."[78] I think we may trace a like development in the attitude of the courts toward the activities of labor unions. The suspicion and even hostility of an earlier generation found reflection in judicial decisions which a changing conception of social values

[78] Knowlton, J., in Anchor Electric Co. v. Hawkes, 171 Mass. 101, 104.

has made it necessary to recast.[79] Some remnants of the older point of view survive, but they are remnants only. The field is one where the law is yet in the making or better perhaps in the re-making. We cannot doubt that its new form will bear an impress of social needs and values which are emerging even now to recognition and to power.

[79] Cf. Laski, "Authority in the Modern State," p. 39.

Lecture III.   The Method of Sociology.   The Judge as a Legislator

I HAVE chosen these branches of the law merely as conspicuous illustrations of the application by the courts of the method of sociology. But the truth is that there is no branch where the method is not fruitful. Even when it does not seem to dominate, it is always in reserve. It is the arbiter between other methods, determining in the last analysis the choice of each, weighing their competing claims, setting bounds to their pretensions, balancing and moderating and harmonizing them all. Few rules in our time are so well established that they may not be called upon any day to justify their existence as means adapted to an end. If they do not function, they are diseased. If they are diseased, they must not propagate their kind. Sometimes they are cut out and extirpated altogether. Sometimes they are left with the shadow of continued life, but sterilized, truncated, impotent for harm.

We get a striking illustration of the force of logical consistency, then of its gradual breaking down before the demands of practical convenience in isolated or exceptional instances, and finally of the generative force of the exceptions as a new stock, in the cases that deal with the right of a beneficiary to recover on a contract. England has been logically consistent and has refused the right of action altogether. New York and most states yielded to the demands of convenience and enforced the right of action, but at first only exceptionally and subject to many restrictions. Gradually the exceptions broadened till today they have left little of the rule.[1] It survives chiefly in those cases where intention would be frustrated or convenience impaired by the extension of the right of action to others than the contracting parties.[2] Rules derived by a process of logical deduction from pre-established

[1] Seaver v. Ransom, 224 N. Y. 233.
[2] Fosmire v. National Surety Co., 229 N. Y. 44.

99

conceptions of contract and obligation have broken down before the slow and steady and erosive action of utility and justice.[3]

We see the same process at work in other fields. We no longer interpret contracts with meticulous adherence to the letter when in conflict with the spirit. We read covenants into them by implication when we find them "instinct with an obligation" imperfectly expressed. "The law has outgrown its primitive stage of formalism when the precise word was the sovereign talisman, and every slip was fatal."[4] Perhaps it is in the field of procedure that we have witnessed the chief changes; though greater ones must yet be wrought. Indictments and civil pleadings are viewed with indulgent eyes. Rulings upon questions of evidence are held with increasing frequency to come within the discretion of the judge presiding at the trial. Errors are no longer ground for the upsetting of judgments with the ensuing horror of new trials, unless the appellate court

[3] Cf. Duguit, *op. cit.*, Continental Legal Hist. Series, vol. XI, p. 120, sec. 36.

[4] Wood v. Duff Gordon, 222 N. Y. 88.

is satisfied that they have affected the result. Legislation has sometimes been necessary to free us from the old fetters. Sometimes the conservatism of judges has threatened for an interval to rob the legislation of its efficacy.[5] This danger was disclosed in the attitude of the courts toward the reforms embodied in codes of practice, in the days when they were first enacted.[6] Precedents established in those times exert an unhappy influence even now. None the less, the tendency today is in the direction of a growing liberalism. The new spirit has made its way gradually; and its progress, unnoticed step by step, is visible in retrospect as we look back upon the distance traversed. The old forms remain, but they are filled with a new content. We are getting away from what Ehrlich calls "die spielerische und die mathematische Entscheidung,"[7] the conception of a lawsuit either as a mathematical prob-

[5] Kelso v. Ellis, 224 N. Y. 528, 536, 537; California Packing Co. v. Kelly S. & D. Co., 228 N. Y. 49.

[6] Pound, "Common Law and Legislation," 21 Harvard L. R. 383, 387.

[7] Ehrlich, "Die juristische Logik," p. 295; cf. pp. 294, 296.

lem or as a sportsman's game. Our own Wigmore has done much to make that conception out of date.[8] We are thinking of the end which the law serves, and fitting its rules to the task of service.

This conception of the end of the law as determining the direction of its growth, which was Jhering's great contribution to the theory of jurisprudence,[9] finds its organon, its instrument, in the method of sociology. Not the origin, but the goal, is the main thing. There can be no wisdom in the choice of a path unless we know where it will lead. The teleological conception of his function must be ever in the judge's mind. This means, of course, that the juristic philosophy of the common law is at bottom the philosophy of pragmatism.[10] Its truth is relative, not absolute. The rule that functions well produces

[8] See his Treatise on Evidence, *passim*.

[9] Jhering, "Zweck im Recht," 5 Modern Legal Philosophy Series; also Gény, *op. cit.*, vol. I, p. 8; Pound, "Scope and Purpose of Sociological Jurisprudence," 25 Harvard L. R. 140, 141, 145; Pound, "Mechanical Jurisprudence," 8 Columbia L. R. 603, 610.

[10] Pound, "Mechanical Jurisprudence," 8 Columbia L. R. 603, 609.

a title deed to recognition. Only in determining how it functions we must not view it too narrowly. We must not sacrifice the general to the particular. We must not throw to the winds the advantages of consistency and uniformity to do justice in the instance.[11] We must keep within those interstitial limits which precedent and custom and the long and silent and almost indefinable practice of other judges through the centuries of the common law have set to judge-made innovations. But within the limits thus set, within the range over which choice moves, the final principle of selection for judges, as for legislators, is one of fitness to an end. "Le but est la vie interne, l'âme cachée, mais génératrice, de tous les droits."[12] We do not pick our rules of law full-blossomed from the trees. Every judge consulting his own experience must be conscious of times when a free exercise of will, directed of

[11] Cf. Brütt, *supra,* pp. 161, 163.

[12] Saleilles, "De la Personnalité Juridique," p. 497.

"Avec Jhering nous resterons des réalistes, mais avec lui aussi nous serons des idéalistes, attachés à l'idée de but et de finalité sociale."—Saleilles, p. 516.

set purpose to the furtherance of the common good, determined the form and tendency of a rule which at that moment took its origin in one creative act. Savigny's conception of law as something realized without struggle or aim or purpose, a process of silent growth, the fruition in life and manners of a people's history and genius, gives a picture incomplete and partial. It is true if we understand it to mean that the judge in shaping the rules of law must heed the *mores* of his day. It is one-sided and therefore false in so far as it implies that the *mores* of the day automatically shape rules which, full grown and ready made, are handed to the judge.[13] Legal norms are confused with legal principles— *Entscheidungsnormen* with *Rechtssätze*.[14] Law is, indeed, an historical growth, for it is an expression of customary morality which develops silently and unconsciously from one age to an-

[13] Cf. Ehrlich, "Grundlegung der Soziologie des Rechts," pp. 366, 368; Pound, "Courts and Legislation," 9 Modern Legal Philosophy Series, p. 212; Gray, "Nature and Sources of Law," secs. 628, 650; Vinogradoff, "Outlines of Historical Jurisprudence," p. 135.

[14] Ehrlich, *supra.*

other. That is the great truth in Savigny's theory of its origin. But law is also a conscious or purposed growth, for the expression of customary morality will be false unless the mind of the judge is directed to the attainment of the moral end and its embodiment in legal forms.[15] Nothing less than conscious effort will be adequate if the end in view is to prevail. The standards or patterns of utility and morals will be found by the judge in the life of the community. They will be found in the same way by the legislator. That does not mean, however, that the work of the one any more than that of the other is a replica of nature's forms.

There has been much debate among foreign jurists whether the norms of right and useful conduct, the patterns of social welfare, are to be found by the judge in conformity with an objective or a subjective standard. Opposing schools of thought have battled for each view.[16] At times,

[15] Cf. Gény, *op. cit.*, vol. I, p. 263, sec. 92.

[16] For a clear and interesting summary, see Brütt, *supra*, p. 101, *et seq.;* cf. Gény, *op. cit.*, vol. I, p. 221; and contrast Flavius, *op. cit.*, p. 87.

the controversy has seemed to turn upon the use of words and little more. So far as the distinction has practical significance, the traditions of our jurisprudence commit us to the objective standard. I do not mean, of course, that this ideal of objective vision is ever perfectly attained. We cannot transcend the limitations of the *ego* and see anything as it really is. None the less, the ideal is one to be striven for within the limits of our capacity. This truth, when clearly perceived, tends to unify the judge's function. His duty to declare the law in accordance with reason and justice is seen to be a phase of his duty to declare it in accordance with custom. It is the customary morality of right-minded men and women which he is to enforce by his decree. A jurisprudence that is not constantly brought into relation to objective or external standards incurs the risk of degenerating into what the Germans call "Die Gefühlsjurisprudenz," a jurisprudence of mere sentiment or feeling.[17] A judical judgment, says Stammler, "should be a judgment of objective

[17] Brütt, *supra*, pp. 101–111.

right, and no subjective and free opinion; a verdict and not a mere personal fiat. Evil stands the case when it is to be said of a judicial decree as the saying goes in the play of the 'Two Gentlemen of Verona' (Act I, sc. ii):

" 'I have no other but a woman's reason;

I think him so, because I think him so.' "[18]

Scholars of distinction have argued for a more subjective standard. "We all agree," says Professor Gray,[19] "that many cases should be decided by the courts on notions of right and wrong, and, of course, everyone will agree that a judge is likely to share the notions of right and wrong prevalent in the community in which he lives; but suppose in a case where there is nothing to guide him but notions of right and wrong, that his notions of right and wrong differ from those of the community—which ought he to follow—his own notions, or the notions of the community? Mr. Carter's theory ["Origin and Sources of Law," J. C. Carter] requires him to

[18] Stammler, "Richtiges Recht," s. 162, quoted by Brütt, *supra,* p. 104.

[19] "Nature and Sources of Law," sec. 610.

say that the judge must follow the notions of the community. I believe that he should follow his own notions." The hypothesis that Professor Gray offers us is not likely to be realized in practice. Rare indeed must be the case when, with conflicting notions of right conduct, there will be nothing else to sway the balance. If, however, the case supposed were here, a judge, I think, would err if he were to impose upon the community as a rule of life his own idiosyncrasies of conduct or belief. Let us suppose, for illustration, a judge who looked upon theatre-going as a sin. Would he be doing right if, in a field where the rule of law was still unsettled, he permitted this conviction, though known to be in conflict with the dominant standard of right conduct, to govern his decision? My own notion is that he would be under a duty to conform to the accepted standards of the community, the *mores* of the times. This does not mean, however, that a judge is powerless to raise the level of prevailing conduct. In one field or another of activity, practices in opposition to the sentiments and standards of the age may grow up and threaten to intrench themselves if not dislodged. Despite their temporary hold, they do not stand comparison with accepted norms of morals. Indolence or passivity has tolerated what the considerate judgment of the community condemns. In such cases, one of the highest functions of the judge is to establish the true relation between conduct and profession. There are even times, to speak somewhat paradoxically, when nothing less than a subjective measure will satisfy objective standards. Some relations in life impose a duty to act in accordance with the customary morality and nothing more. In those the customary morality must be the standard for the judge. *Caveat emptor* is a maxim that will often have to be followed when the morality which it expresses is not that of sensitive souls. Other relations in life, as, e.g., those of trustee and beneficiary, or principal and surety, impose a duty to act in accordance with the highest standards which a man of the most delicate conscience and the nicest sense of honor might impose upon himself. In such cases, to enforce adherence to those standards becomes the duty of the judge. Whether novel situations are to be brought within one class of relations or within the other must be determined, as they arise, by considerations of analogy, of convenience, of fitness, and of justice.

The truth, indeed, is, as I have said, that the distinction between the subjective or individual and the objective or general conscience, in the field where the judge is not limited by established rules, is shadowy and evanescent, and tends to become one of words and little more. For the casuist and the philosopher, it has its speculative interest. In the practical administration of justice, it will seldom be decisive for the judge. This is admitted by Brütt, one of the staunchest upholders of the theory of objective right.[20] The perception of objective right takes the color of the subjective mind. The conclusions of the subjective mind take the color of customary practices and objectified beliefs. There is con-

[20] *Supra,* p. 139.

stant and subtle interaction between what is without and what is within. We may hold, on the one side, with Tarde and his school, that all social innovations come "from individual inventions spread by imitation,"[21] or on the other side, with Durkheim and his school, that all such innovations come "through the action of the social mind."[22] In either view, whether the impulse spreads from the individual or from society, from within or from without, neither the components nor the mass can work in independence of each other. The personal and the general mind and will are inseparably united. The difference, as one theory of judicial duty or the other prevails, involves at most a little change of emphasis, of the method of approach, of the point of view, the angle, from which problems are envisaged. Only dimly and by force of an influence subconscious, or nearly so, will the difference be reflected in the decisions of the courts.

[21] Barnes, "Durkheim's Political Theory," 35 **Pol.** Science Quarterly, p. 239.

[22] *Ibid.;* cf. Barker, "Political Thought from **Spencer** to Today," pp. 151, 153, 175.

THE JUDGE AS A LEGISLATOR

My analysis of the judicial process comes then to this, and little more: logic, and history, and custom, and utility, and the accepted standards of right conduct, are the forces which singly or in combination shape the progress of the law. Which of these forces shall dominate in any case must depend largely upon the comparative importance or value of the social interests that will be thereby promoted or impaired.[23] One of the most fundamental social interests is that law shall be uniform and impartial. There must be nothing in its action that savors of prejudice or favor or even arbitrary whim or fitfulness. Therefore in the main there shall be adherence to precedent. There shall be symmetrical development, consistently with history or custom when history or custom has been the motive force, or the chief one, in giving shape to existing rules, and with logic or philosophy when the motive power has been theirs. But symmetrical development may be bought at too high a price. Uni-

[23] Vander Eycken, "Méthode Positive de l'Interprétation juridique," p. 59; Ehrlich, "Die juristische Logik," p. 187.

formity ceases to be a good when it becomes uniformity of oppression. The social interest served by symmetry or certainty must then be balanced against the social interest served by equity and fairness or other elements of social welfare. These may enjoin upon the judge the duty of drawing the line at another angle, of staking the path along new courses, of marking a new point of departure from which others who come after him will set out upon their journey.

If you ask how he is to know when one interest outweighs another, I can only answer that he must get his knowledge just as the legislator gets it, from experience and study and reflection; in brief, from life itself. Here, indeed, is the point of contact between the legislator's work and his. The choice of methods, the appraisement of values, must in the end be guided by like considerations for the one as for the other. Each indeed is legislating within the limits of his competence. No doubt the limits for the judge are narrower. He legislates only between gaps. He fills the open spaces in the law. How far he

may go without traveling beyond the walls of
the interstices cannot be staked out for him
upon a chart. He must learn it for himself as he
gains the sense of fitness and proportion that
comes with years of habitude in the practice of
an art. Even within the gaps, restrictions not
easy to define, but felt, however impalpable they
may be, by every judge and lawyer, hedge and
circumscribe his action. They are established by
the traditions of the centuries, by the example
of other judges, his predecessors and his col-
leagues, by the collective judgment of the profession, and by the duty of adherence to the
pervading spirit of the law. "Il ne peut inter-
venir," says Charmont,[24] "que pour suppléer les
sources formelles, mais il n'a pas, dans cette
mesure même, toute latitude pour créer des
règles de droit. Il ne peut ni faire échec aux
principes généraux de notre organisation juridique, explicitement on implicitement consacrés,
ni formuler une réglementation de detail pour
l'exercise de certains droits, en établissant des

[24] "La Renaissance du droit naturel," p. 181.

114

délais, des formalités, des règles de publicité."[25]
None the less, within the confines of these open
spaces and those of precedent and tradition,
choice moves with a freedom which stamps its
action as creative. The law which is the resulting
product is not found, but made. The process,
being legislative, demands the legislator's wisdom.

[25] "He may intervene only to supplement the formal
authorities, and even in that field there are limits to his
discretion in establishing rules of law. He may neither
restrict the scope of the general principles of our juridical organization, explicitly or implicitly sanctioned, nor
may he lay down detailed regulations governing the
exercise of given rights, by introducing delays,
formalities, or rules of publicity."—Charmont, *supra,*
transl. in 7 Modern Legal Philosophy Series, p. 120, sec.
91. Cf. Jhering, "Law as a Means to an End" (5 Modern
Legal Philosophy Series: Introduction by W. M. Gel-
dart, p. xlvi): "The purposes of law are embodied in
legal conceptions which must develop in independence and cannot at every step be called upon to
conform to particular needs. Otherwise system and
certainty would be unattainable. But this autonomy of
law, if it were only because of excess or defects of
logic, will lead to a divergence between law and the
needs of life, which from time to time calls for correc-
tion. . . . How far if at all the needful changes can
or ought to be carried out by judicial decisions or the
development of legal theory, and how far the interven-
tion of the legislator will be called for, is a matter that
will vary from one legal territory to another according
to the accepted traditions as to the binding force of

There is in truth nothing revolutionary or even novel in this view of the judicial function.[26] It is the way that courts have gone about their business for centuries in the development of the common law. The difference from age to age is not so much in the recognition of the need that law shall conform itself to an end. It is rather in the nature of the end to which there has been need to conform. There have been periods when uniformity, even rigidity, the elimination of the personal element, were felt to be the paramount needs.[27] By a sort of paradox, the end was best served by disregarding it and thinking only of the means. Gradually the need of a more flexible system asserted itself. Often the gap between the old rule and the new was bridged by the pious fraud of a fiction.[28] The thing which concerns us here is that it was bridged whenever the

precedents, the character of the enacted law, and the wider or narrower liberty of judicial interpretation."

[26] Cf. Berolzheimer, 9 Modern Legal Philosophy Series, pp. 167, 168.

[27] Flavius, *supra*, p. 49; 2 Pollock and Maitland, "History of English Law," p. 561.

[28] Smith, "Surviving Fictions," 27 Yale L. J., 147,

importance of the end was dominant. Today the use of fictions has declined; and the springs of action are disclosed where once they were concealed. Even now, they are not fully known, however, even to those whom they control. Much of the process has been unconscious or nearly so. The ends to which courts have addressed themselves, the reasons and motives that have guided them, have often been vaguely felt, intuitively or almost intuitively apprehended, seldom explicitly avowed. There has been little of deliberate introspection, of dissection, of analysis, of philosophizing. The result has been an amalgam of which the ingredients were unknown or forgotten. That is why there is something of a shock in the discovery that legislative policy has made the compound what it is. "We do not

317; Ehrlich, *supra,* pp. 227, 228; Saleilles, "De la Pérsonnalité Juridique," p. 382.

"Lorsque la loi sanctionne certains rapports juridiques, à l'exclusion de tels autres qui en différent, il arrive, pour tels ou tels rapports de droit plus ou moins similaires auxquels on sent le besoin d'étendre la protection légale, que l'on est tenté de procéder, soit par analogie, soit par fiction. La fiction est une analogie un peu amplifiée, ou plutôt non dissimulée."—Saleilles, *supra.*

realize," says Holmes,[29] "how large a part of our law is open to reconsideration upon a slight change in the habit of the public mind. No concrete proposition is self-evident, no matter how ready we may be to accept it, not even Mr. Herbert Spencer's every man has a right to do what he wills, provided he interferes not with a like right on the part of his neighbors." "Why," he continues, "is a false and injurious statement privileged, if it is made honestly in giving information about a servant? It is because it has been thought more important that information should be given freely, than that a man should be protected from what under other circumstances would be an actionable wrong. Why is a man at liberty to set up a business which he knows will ruin his neighbor? It is because the public good is supposed to be best subserved by free competition. Obviously such judgments of relative importance may vary in different times and places. . . . I think that the judges themselves have failed adequately to recognize their

[29] "The Path of the Law," 10 Harvard L. R. 466.

duty of weighing considerations of social advantage. The duty is inevitable, and the result of the often proclaimed judicial aversion to deal with such considerations is simply to leave the very ground and foundation of judgments inarticulate, and often unconscious, as I have said."

Not only in our common law system has this conception made its way. Even in other systems where the power of judicial initiative is more closely limited by stature, a like development is in the air. Everywhere there is growing emphasis on the analogy between the function of the judge and the function of the legislator. I may instance François Gény who has developed the analogy with boldness and suggestive power.[30] "A priori," he says, "the process of research (*la recherche*), which is imposed upon the judge in finding the law seems to us very analogous to that incumbent on the legislator himself. Except for this circumstance, certainly not negligible, and yet of secondary importance, that the process

[30] *Op. cit.*, vol. II, p. 77.

is set in motion by some concrete situation, and in order to adapt the law to that situation, the considerations which ought to guide it are, in respect of the final end to be attained, exactly of the same nature as those which ought to dominate legislative action itself, since it is a question in each case, of satisfying, as best may be, justice and social utility by an appropriate rule. Hence, I will not hesitate in the silence or inadequacy of formal sources, to indicate as the general line of direction for the judge the following: that he ought to shape his judgment of the law in obedience to the same aims which would be those of a legislator who was proposing to himself to regulate the question. None the less, an important distinction separates here judicial from legislative activity. While the legislator is not hampered by any limitations in the appreciation of a general situation, which he regulates in a manner altogether abstract, the judge, who decides in view of particular cases, and with reference to problems absolutely concrete, ought, in adherence to the spirit of our modern organization, and in order to escape the dangers of arbitrary action, to disengage himself, so far as possible, of every influence that is personal or that comes from the particular situation which is presented to him, and base his judicial decision on elements of an objective nature. And that is why the activity which is proper to him has seemed to me capable of being justly qualified: free scientific research, *libre recherche scientifique:* free, since it is here removed from the action of positive authority; scientific, at the same time, because it can find its solid foundations only in the objective elements which science alone is able to reveal to it."[31]

The rationale of the modern viewpoint has been admirably expressed by Vander Eycken[32] in his "Méthode positive de l'Interprétation juridique":[33] "Formerly men looked upon law as the product of the conscious will of the legislator. Today they see in it a natural force.

[31] Ehrlich has the same thought, "Die juristische Logik," p. 312.
[32] Professor in the University of Brussels.
[33] P. 401, sec. 239.

If, however, we can attribute to law the epithet 'natural,' it is, as we have said, in a different sense from that which formerly attached to the expression 'natural law.' That expression then meant that nature had imprinted in us, as one of the very elements of reason, certain principles of which all the articles of the code were only the application. The same expression ought to mean today that law springs from the relations of fact which exist between things. Like those relations themselves, natural law is in perpetual travail. It is no longer in texts or in systems derived from reason that we must look for the source of law; it is in social utility, in the necessity that certain consequences shall be attached to given hypotheses. The legislator has only a fragmentary consciousness of this law; he translates it by the rules which he prescribes. When the question is one of fixing the meaning of those rules, where ought we to search? Manifestly at their source; that is to say, in the exigencies of social life. There resides the strongest probability of discovering the sense of the law. In the same way when the question is one of supplying the gaps in the law, it is not of logical deductions, it is rather of social needs, that we are to ask the solution."

Many of the gaps have been filled in the development of the common law by borrowing from other systems. Whole titles in our jurisprudence have been taken from the law of Rome. Some of the greatest of our judges—Mansfield in England, Kent and Story here—were never weary of supporting their judgments by citations from the Digest. We should be traveling too far afield if we were to attempt an estimate of the extent to which the law of Rome has modified the common law either in England or with us.[34] Authority it never had. The great historic movement of the Reception did not touch the British Isles.[35] Analogies have been supplied. Lines of thought have been suggested. Wise solutions

[34] On this subject, see Sherman, "Roman Law in the Modern World"; Scrutton, "Roman Law Influence," 1 Select Essays in Anglo-Am. Legal Hist. 208.

[35] 1 Pollock and Maitland's "History of English Law," 88, 114; Maitland's "Introduction to Gierke," *supra*, p. xii.

have been offered for problems otherwise insoluble. None the less, the function of the foreign system has been to advise rather than to command. It has not furnished a new method. It has given the raw material to be utilized by methods already considered—the methods of philosophy and history and sociology—in the moulding of their products. It is only one compartment in the great reservoir of social experience and truth and wisdom from which the judges of the common law must draw their inspiration and their knowledge.

In thus recognizing, as I do, that the power to declare the law carries with it the power, and within limits the duty, to make law when none exists, I do not mean to range myself with the jurists who seem to hold that in reality there is no law except the decisions of the courts. I think the truth is midway between the extremes that are represented at one end by Coke and Hale and Blackstone and at the other by such authors as Austin and Holland and Gray and Jethro Brown. The theory of the older writers was that judges did not legislate at all. A pre-existing rule was there, imbedded, if concealed, in the body of the customary law. All that the judges did was to throw off the wrappings, and expose the statue to our view.[36] Since the days of Bentham and Austin, no one, it is believed, has accepted this theory without deduction or reserve, though even in modern decisions we find traces of its lingering influence. Today there is rather danger of another though an opposite error. From holding that the law is never made by judges, the votaries of the Austinian analysis have been led at times to the conclusion that it is never made by anyone else. Customs, no matter how firmly established, are not law, they say, until adopted by the courts.[37] Even statutes are not law because the courts must fix their meaning. That is the view of Gray in his "Nature and Sources of the Law."[38] "The true view, as I

[36] Cf. Pound, 27 Harvard L. R. 731, 733.

[37] Austin, "Jurisprudence," vol. I, 37, 104; Holland, "Jurisprudence," p. 54; W. Jethro Brown, "The Austinian Theory of Law," p. 311.

[38] Sec. 602.

submit," he says, "is that the Law is what the Judges declare; that statutes, precedents, the opinions of learned experts, customs and morality are the sources of the Law."[39] So, Jethro Brown in a paper on "Law and Evolution,"[40] tells us that a statute, till construed, is not real law. It is only "ostensible" law. Real law, he says, is not found anywhere except in the judgment of a court. In that view, even past decisions are not law. The courts may overrule them. For the same reason present decisions are not law, except for the parties litigant. Men go about their business from day to day, and govern their conduct by an *ignis fatuus*. The rules to which they yield obedience are in truth not law at all. Law never *is*, but is always about to be. It is realized only when embodied in a judgment, and in being realized, expires. There are no such things as rules or principles: there are only isolated dooms.

A definition of law which in effect denies the possibility of law since it denies the possibility of

[39] Cf. Gray, *supra*, secs. 276, 366, 369.
[40] 29 Yale L. J. 394.

rules of general operation [41] must contain within itself the seeds of fallacy and error. Analysis is useless if it destroys what it is intended to explain. Law and obedience to law are facts confirmed every day to us all in our experience of life. If the result of a definition is to make them seem to be illusions, so much the worse for the definition; we must enlarge it till it is broad enough to answer to realities. The outstanding truths of life, the great and unquestioned phenomena of society, are not to be argued away as myths and vagaries when they do not fit within our little moulds. If necessary, we must remake the moulds. We must seek a conception of law which realism can accept as true. Statutes do not cease to be law because the power to fix their meaning in case of doubt or ambiguity has been confided to the courts. One might as well say for like reasons that contracts have no reality as expressions of a contracting will. The quality of law is not withdrawn from all precedents, however well established, because courts

[41] Cf. Beale, "Conflict of Laws," p. 153, sec. 129.

sometimes exercise the privilege of overruling their own decisions. Those, I think, are the conclusions to which a sense of realism must lead us. No doubt there is a field within which judicial judgment moves untrammeled by fixed principles. Obscurity of statute or of precedent or of customs or of morals, or collision between some or all of them, may leave the law unsettled, and cast a duty upon the courts to declare it retrospectively in the exercise of a power frankly legislative in function. In such cases, all that the parties to the controversy can do is to forecast the declaration of the rule as best they can, and govern themselves accordingly. We must not let these occasional and relatively rare instances blind our eyes to the innumerable instances where there is neither obscurity nor collision nor opportunity for diverse judgment. Most of us live our lives in conscious submission to rules of law, yet without necessity of resort to the courts to ascertain our rights and duties. Lawsuits are rare and catastrophic experiences for the vast majority of men, and even when the catastrophe ensues, the controversy relates most often not to the law, but to the facts. In countless litigations, the law is so clear that judges have no discretion. They have the right to legislate within gaps, but often there are no gaps. We shall have a false view of the landscape if we look at the waste spaces only, and refuse to see the acres already sown and fruitful. I think the difficulty has its origin in the failure to distinguish between right and power, between the command embodied in a judgment and the jural principle to which the obedience of the judge is due. Judges have, of course, the power, though not the right, to ignore the mandate of a statute, and render judgment in despite of it. They have the power, though not the right, to travel beyond the walls of the interstices, the bounds set to judicial innovation by precedent and custom. None the less, by that abuse of power, they violate the law. If they violate it willfully, i.e., with guilty and evil mind, they commit a legal wrong, and may be removed or punished even though the judgments which they have rendered stand.

In brief, there are jural principles which limit the freedom of the judge,[42] and, indeed, in the view of some writers, which we do not need to endorse, the freedom of the state itself.[43] Life may be lived, conduct may be ordered, it *is* lived and ordered, for unnumbered human beings without bringing them within the field where the law can be misread, unless indeed the misreading be accompanied by conscious abuse of power. Their conduct never touches the borderland, the penumbra, where controversy begins. They go from birth to death, their action restrained at every turn by the power of the state, and not once do they appeal to judges to mark the boundaries between right and wrong. I am unable to withhold the name of law from rules which exercise this compulsion over the fortunes of mankind.[44]

[42] Salmond, "Jurisprudence," p. 157; Sadler, "Relation of Law to Custom," pp. 4, 6, 50; F. A. Geer, 9 L. Q. R. 153.

[43] Duguit, "Law and the State," 31 Harvard L. R. 1; Vinogradoff, "The Crisis of Modern Jurisprudence," 29 Yale L. J. 312; Laski, "Authority in the Modern State," pp. 41, 42.

[44] "Law is the body of general principles and of

THE JUDGE AS A LEGISLATOR

The old Blackstonian theory of pre-existing rules of law which judges found, but did not make, fitted in with a theory still more ancient, the theory of a law of nature. The growth of that conception forms a long and interesting chapter in the history of jurisprudence and political science.[45] The doctrine reached its highest development with the Stoics, has persisted in varying phases through the centuries, and imbedding itself deeply in common forms of speech and thought, has profoundly influenced the speculations and ideals of men in statecraft and in law. For a time, with the rise and dominance of the analytical school of jurists, it seemed discredited and abandoned.[46] Recent juristic thought has given it a new currency, though in a form so profoundly altered that the old theory survives

particular rules in accordance with which civil rights are created and regulated, and wrongs prevented or redressed" (Beale, "Conflict of Laws," p. 132, sec. 114).

[45] Salmond, "The Law of Nature," 11 L. Q. R. 121; Pollock, "The History of the Law of Nature," 1 Columbia L. R. 11; 2 Lowell, "The Government of England," 477, 478; Maitland's "Collected Papers," p. 23.

[46] Cf. Ritchie, "Natural Rights."

in little more than name.[47] The law of nature is no longer conceived of as something static and eternal. It does not override human or positive law. It is the stuff out of which human or positive law is to be woven, when other sources fail.[48] "The modern philosophy of law comes in contact with the natural law philosophy in that the one as well as the other seeks to be the science of the just. But the modern philosophy of law departs essentially from the natural-law philosophy in that the latter seeks a just, natural law outside of positive law, while the new philosophy of law desires to deduce and fix the element of the just in and out of the positive law—out of what it is and of what it is becoming. The natural law school seeks an absolute, ideal law, 'natural law,' the law κατ᾽ ἐξοχῆν, by the side of which positive law has only secondary importance. The

[47] Pound, 25 Harvard L. R. 162; Charmont, "La Renaissance du droit naturel," *passim;* also transl., 7 Modern Legal Philosophy Series, pp. 106, 111; Demogue, "Analysis of Fundamental Notions," 7 Modern Legal Philosophy Series, p. 373, sec. 212; Laski, "Authority in the Modern State," p. 64.

[48] Vander Eycken, *op. cit.,* p. 401.

modern philosophy of law recognizes that there is only *one* law, the positive law, but it seeks its ideal side, and its enduring idea."[49] I am not concerned to vindicate the accuracy of the nomenclature by which the dictates of reason and conscience which the judge is under a duty to obey are given the name of law before he has embodied them in a judgment and set the *imprimatur* of the law upon them.[50] I shall not be troubled if we say with Austin and Holland and Gray and many others that till then they are moral precepts, and nothing more. Such verbal disputations do not greatly interest me. What really matters is this, that the judge is under a duty, within the limits of his power of innovation, to maintain a relation between law and morals, between the precepts of jurisprudence

[49] Berolzheimer, "System der Rechts und Wirthschaftsphilosophie," vol. II, 27, quoted by Pound, "Scope and Purpose of Sociological Jurisprudence," 24 Harvard L. R. 607; also Isaacs, "The Schools of Jurisprudence," 31 Harvard L. R. 373, 389; and for the mediaeval view, Maitland's "Gierke, Political Theories of the Middle Age," pp. 75, 84, 93, 173.

[50] Holland, "Jurisprudence," p. 54.

and those of reason and good conscience. I suppose it is true in a certain sense that this duty was never doubted.[51] One feels at times, however, that it was obscured by the analytical jurists, who, in stressing verbal niceties of definition, made a corresponding sacrifice of emphasis upon the deeper and finer realities of ends and aims and functions. The constant insistence that morality and justice are not law has tended to breed distrust and contempt of law as something to which morality and justice are not merely alien, but hostile. The new development of "naturrecht" may be pardoned infelicities of phrase, if it introduces us to new felicities of methods and ideals. Not for us the barren logomachy that dwells upon the contrasts between law and justice, and forgets their deeper harmonies. For us rather the trumpet call of the French "code civil":[52] "Le juge, qui refusera de juger, sous prétexte du silence, de l'obscurité

[51] See Gray, *supra*, p. 286, secs. 644, 645.

[52] Art. 4; Gray, *supra*, sec. 642; Gény, *op. cit.*, vol. II, p. 75, sec. 155; Gnaeus Flavius, "Der Kampf um die Rechtswissenschaft," p. 14.

ou de l'insuffisance de la loi, pourra être poursuivi comme coupable de déni de justice."[53] "It is the function of our courts," says an acute critic, "to keep the doctrines up to date with the *mores* by continual restatement and by giving them a continually new content. This is judicial legislation, and the judge legislates at his peril. Nevertheless, it is the necessity and duty of such legislation that gives to judicial office its highest honor; and no brave and honest judge shirks the duty or fears the peril."[54]

You may say that there is no assurance that judges will interpret the *mores* of their day more wisely and truly than other men. I am not disposed to deny this, but in my view it is quite beside the point. The point is rather that this power of interpretation must be lodged somewhere, and the custom of the constitution has lodged it in the judges. If they are to fulfill their

[53] "The judge who shall refuse to give judgment under pretext of the silence, of the obscurity, or of the inadequacy of the law, shall be subject to prosecution as guilty of a denial of justice."

[54] Arthur L. Corbin, 29 Yale L. J. 771.

function as judges, it could hardly be lodged elsewhere. Their conclusions must, indeed, be subject to constant testing and retesting, revision and readjustment; but if they act with conscience and intelligence, they ought to attain in their conclusions a fair average of truth and wisdom. The recognition of this power and duty to shape the law in conformity with the customary morality is something far removed from the destruction of all rules and the substitution in every instance of the individual sense of justice, the *arbitrium boni viri*.[55] That might result in a benevolent despotism if the judges were benevolent men. It would put an end to the reign of law. The method of sociology, even though applied with greater freedom than in the past, is heading us toward no such cataclysm. The form and structure of the organism are fixed. The cells in which there is motion do not change the proportions of the mass. Insignificant is the power of innovation of any judge, when compared with

[55] Cf. Standard Chemical Corp. v. Waugh Corp., 231 N. Y. 51, 55.

the bulk and pressure of the rules that hedge him on every side. Innovate, however, to some extent, he must, for with new conditions there must be new rules. All that the method of sociology demands is that within this narrow range of choice he shall search for social justice. There were stages in the history of the law when a method less psychological was needed. The old quantitative tests of truth did not fail in their day to serve the social needs.[56] Their day has long passed. Modern juristic thought, turning in upon itself, subjecting the judicial process to introspective scrutiny, may have given us a new terminology and a new emphasis. But in truth its method is not new. It is the method of the great chancellors, who without sacrificing uniformity and certainty built up the system of equity with constant appeal to the teachings of right reason and conscience. It is the method by which the common law has renewed its life at

[56] Flavius, "Der Kampf um die Rechtswissenschaft," pp. 48, 49; Ehrlich, "Die juristische Logik," pp. 291, 292.

the hands of its great masters—the method of Mansfield and Marshall and Kent and Holmes.

There have, indeed, been movements, and in our own day, to make the individual sense of justice in law as well as in morals the sole criterion of right and wrong. We are invited, in Gény's phrase, to establish a system of "juridical anarchy" at worst, or of "judicial impressionism" at best.[57] The experiment, or something at least approaching it, was tried not long ago in France. There are sponsors of a like creed among the critics of our own courts.[58] The French experiment, which has become known as "le phénomène Magnaud," is the subject of a chapter in the epilogue to the last edition, published in 1919, of Gény's brilliant book.[59] Between 1889 and 1904, the tribunal of the first

[57] Gény, *op. cit.*, ed. of 1919, vol. II, p. 288, sec. 196; p. 305, sec. 200.

[58] Bruce, "Judicial Buncombe in North Dakota and Other States," 88 Central L. J. 136; Judge Robinson's Reply, 88 *ibid.* 155; "Rule and Discretion in the Administration of Justice," 33 Harvard L. R. 792.

[59] Gény, *op. cit.*, ed. of 1919, vol. II, p. 287, sec. 196, *et seq.*

instance of Château-Thierry, following the lead of its chief, le President Magnaud, initiated a revolt against the existing order in jurisprudence. Its members became known as the good judges, *"les bons juges."* They seem to have asked themselves in every instance what in the circumstances before them a good man would wish to do, and to have rendered judgment accordingly. Sometimes this was done in the face of inconsistent statutes. I do not profess to know their work at first hand. Gény condemns it, and says the movement has spent its force. Whatever the merits or demerits of such impressionism may be, that is not the judicial process as we know it in our law.[60] Our jurisprudence has held fast to Kant's categorical imperative, "Act on a maxim which thou canst will to be law universal." It has refused to sacrifice the larger and more inclusive good to the narrower and smaller. A contract is made. Performance is burdensome and perhaps oppressive. If we were to consider only the individual instance, we might be ready to

[60] Salmond, "Jurisprudence," pp. 19, 20.

release the promisor. We look beyond the particular to the universal, and shape our judgment in obedience to the fundamental interest of society that contracts shall be fulfilled. There is a wide gap between the use of the individual sentiment of justice as a substitute for law, and its use as one of the tests and touchstones in construing or extending law. I think the tone and temper in which the modern judge should set about his task are well expressed in the first article of the Swiss Civil Code of 1907, an article around which there has grown up a large body of juristic commentary. "The statute," says the Swiss Code, "governs all matters within the letter or the spirit of any of its mandates. In default of an applicable statute, the judge is to pronounce judgment according to the customary law, and in default of a custom according to the rules which he would establish if he were to assume the part of a legislator. He is to draw his inspiration, however, from the solutions consecrated by the doctrine of the learned and the jurisprudence of the courts—par la doctrine et la jurisprudence."[61] There, in the final precept, is the gist of the difference between "le phé-nomène Magnaud," and justice according to law. The judge, even when he is free, is still not wholly free. He is not to innovate at pleasure. He is not a knight-errant roaming at will in pursuit of his own ideal of beauty or of goodness. He is to draw his inspiration from consecrated principles. He is not to yield to spasmodic senti-ment, to vague and unregulated benevolence. He is to exercise a discretion informed by tradi-tion, methodized by analogy, disciplined by sys-tem, and subordinated to "the primordial neces-sity of order in the social life."[62] Wide enough in all conscience is the field of discretion that remains.

[61] Gény, *op. cit.*, II, p. 213; also Perick, "The Swiss Code," XI, Continental Legal Hist. Series, p. 238, sec. 5.
[62] Gény, *op. cit.*, II, p. 303, sec. 200.

Lecture IV. Adherence to Precedent. The Subconscious Element in the Judicial Process. Conclusion.

THE system of law-making by judicial decisions which supply the rule for transactions closed before the decision was announced would indeed be intolerable in its hardship and oppression if natural law, in the sense in which I have used the term, did not supply the main rule of judgment to the judge when precedent and custom fail or are displaced. Acquiescence in such a method has its basis in the belief that when the law has left the situation uncovered by any pre-existing rule, there is nothing to do except to have some impartial arbiter declare what fair and reasonable men, mindful of the habits of life of the community, and of the standards of justice and fair dealing prevalent among them, ought in such circumstances to do, with no rules except those of custom and conscience to regulate their conduct. The feeling is that nine times out of ten, if not oftener, the conduct of right-minded men would not have been different if the rule embodied in the decision had been announced by statute in advance. In the small minority of cases, where ignorance has counted, it is as likely to have affected one side as the other; and since a controversy has arisen and must be determined somehow, there is nothing to do, in default of a rule already made, but to constitute some authority which will make it after the event. Some one must be the loser; it is part of the game of life; we have to pay in countless ways for the absence of prophetic vision. No doubt the ideal system, if it were attainable, would be a code at once so flexible and so minute, as to supply in advance for every conceivable situation the just and fitting rule. But life is too complex to bring the attainment of this ideal within the compass of human powers. We must recognize the truth, says Gény,[1] that the will (*la volonté*) which inspires a statute

[1] *Op. cit.*, Preface, p. xvi.

"extends only over a domain of concrete facts, very narrow and very limited. Almost always, a statute has only a single point in view. All history demonstrates that legislation intervenes only when a definite abuse has disclosed itself, through the excess of which public feeling has finally been aroused. When the legislator interposes, it is to put an end to such and such facts, very clearly determined, which have provoked his decision. And if, to reach his goal, he thinks it proper to proceed along the path of general ideas and abstract formulas, the principles that he announces have value, in his thought, only in the measure in which they are applicable to the evils which it was his effort to destroy, and to similar conditions which would tend to spring from them. As for other logical consequences to be deduced from these principles, the legislator has not suspected them; some, perhaps many, if he had foreseen, he would not have hesitated to repudiate. In consecrating them, no one can claim either to be following his will or to be bowing to his judgment. All that one does thereby is to develop a principle, henceforth isolated and independent of the will which created it, to transform it into a new entity, which in turn develops of itself, and to give it an independent life, regardless of the will of the legislator and most often in despite of it." These are the words of a French jurist, writing of a legal system founded on a code. The gaps inevitable in such a system must, at least in equal measure, be inevitable in a system of case law built up, haphazard, through the controversies of litigants.[2] In each system, hardship must at times result from postponement of the rule of action till a time when action is complete. It is one of the consequences of the limitations of the human intellect and of the denial to legislators and judges of infinite prevision. But the truth is, as I have said, that even when there is ignorance of the rule, the cases are few in which ignorance has determined conduct. Most often the controversy arises about something that would

[2] Pollack, "Essays in Jurisprudence and Ethics; The Science of Case Law," p. 241.

have happened anyhow. An automobile is manufactured with defective wheels. The question is whether the manufacturer owes a duty of inspection to anyone except the buyer.[3] The occupant of the car, injured because of the defect, presses one view upon the court; the manufacturer, another. There is small chance, whichever party prevails, that conduct would have been different if the rule had been known in advance. The manufacturer did not say to himself, "I will not inspect these wheels, because that is not my duty." Admittedly, it was his duty, at least toward the immediate buyer. A wrong in any event has been done. The question is to what extent it shall entail unpleasant consequences on the wrongdoer.

I say, therefore, that in the vast majority of cases the retrospective effect of judge-made law is felt either to involve no hardship or only such hardship as is inevitable where no rule has been declared. I think it is significant that when the hardship is felt to be too great or to be un-

[3] MacPherson v. Buick Motor Co., 217 N. Y. 382.

necessary, retrospective operation is withheld. Take the cases where a court of final appeal has declared a statute void, and afterward, reversing itself, declares the statute valid. Intervening transactions have been governed by the first decision. What shall be said of the validity of such transactions when the decision is overruled? Most courts in a spirit of realism have held that the operation of the statute has been suspended in the interval.[4] It may be hard to square such a ruling with abstract dogmas and definitions. When so much else that a court does is done with retroactive force, why draw the line here? The answer is, I think, that the line is drawn here, because the injustice and oppression of a refusal to draw it would be so great as to be intolerable. We will not help out the man who has

[4] Harris v. Jex, 55 N. Y. 421; Gelpcke v. Dubuque, 1 Wall. 125; Holmes, J., in Kuhn v. Fairmount Coal Co., 215 U. S. 349, 371; 29 Harvard L. R. 80, 103; Danchey Co. v. Farmy, 105 Misc. 470; Freeman, "Retroactive Operation of Decisions," 18 Columbia L. R. p. 230; Gray, *supra*, secs. 547, 548; Carpenter, "Court Decisions and the Common Law," 17 Columbia L. R. 593.

trusted to the judgment of some inferior court.[5] In his case, the chance of miscalculation is felt to be a fair risk of the game of life, not different in degree from the risk of any other misconception of right or duty. He knows that he has taken a chance, which caution often might have avoided. The judgment of a court of final appeal is felt to stand upon a different basis. I am not sure that any adequate distinction is to be drawn between a change of ruling in respect of the validity of a statute and a change of ruling in respect of the meaning or operation of a statute,[6] or even in respect of the meaning or operation of a rule of common law.[7] Where the line of division will some day be located, I will make no attempt to say. I feel assured, however, that its location, wherever it shall be, will be governed, not by metaphysical conceptions of the nature of judge-made law, nor by the fetich of some implacable tenet, such as that of the division of

[5] Evans v. Supreme Council, 223 N. Y. 497, 503.

[6] Douglass v. County of Pike, 101 U. S. 677.

[7] Cf. Wigmore, "The Judicial Function," Preface to 9 Modern Legal Philosophy Series, pp. xxxvii, xxxviii.

governmental powers,[8] but by considerations of convenience, of utility, and of the deepest sentiments of justice.

In these days, there is a good deal of discussion whether the rule of adherence to precedent ought to be abandoned altogether.[9] I would not go so far myself. I think adherence to precedent should be the rule and not the exception. I have already had occasion to dwell upon some of the considerations that sustain it. To these I may add that the labor of judges would be increased almost to the breaking point if every past decision could be reopened in every case, and one could not lay one's own course of bricks on the secure foundation of the courses laid by others who had gone before him. Perhaps the constitution of my own court has tended to accentuate this belief. We have had ten judges, of whom

[8] Laski, "Authority in the Modern State," pp. 70, 71; Green, "Separation of Governmental Powers," 29 Yale L. J. 371.

[9] "Rule and Discretion in the Administration of Justice," 33 Harvard L. R. 972; 29 Yale L. J. 909; 34 Harvard L. R. 74; 9 Modern Legal Philosophy Series, Preface, p. xxxvi.

only seven sit at a time. It happens again and again, where the question is a close one, that a case which one week is decided one way might be decided another way the next if it were then heard for the first time. The situation would, however, be intolerable if the weekly changes in the composition of the court were accompanied by changes in its rulings. In such circumstances there is nothing to do except to stand by the errors of our brethren of the week before, whether we relish them or not. But I am ready to concede that the rule of adherence to precedent, though it ought not to be abandoned, ought to be in some degree relaxed. I think that when a rule, after it has been duly tested by experience, has been found to be inconsistent with the sense of justice or with the social welfare, there should be less hesitation in frank avowal and full abandonment. We have had to do this sometimes in the field of constitutional law.[10] Perhaps we should do so oftener in fields of private law where considerations of social utility are not so

[10] Klein v. Maravelas, 219 N. Y. 383.

aggressive and insistent. There should be greater readiness to abandon an untenable position when the rule to be discarded may not reasonably be supposed to have determined the conduct of the litigants, and particularly when in its origin it was the product of institutions or conditions which have gained a new significance or development with the progress of the years. In such circumstances, the words of Wheeler, J., in Dwy v. Connecticut Co., 89 Conn. 74, 99, express the tone and temper in which problems should be met: "That court best serves the law which recognizes that the rules of law which grew up in a remote generation may, in the fullness of experience, be found to serve another generation badly, and which discards the old rule when it finds that another rule of law represents what should be according to the established and settled judgment of society, and no considerable property rights have become vested in reliance upon the old rule. It is thus great writers upon the common law have discovered the source and method of its growth, and in its growth found its health and life. It is not and it should not be stationary. Change of this character should not be left to the legislature." If judges have wofully misinterpreted the *mores* of their day, or if the *mores* of their day are no longer those of ours, they ought not to tie, in helpless submission, the hands of their successors.

Let me offer one or two examples to make my meaning plainer. I offer them tentatively and without assurance that they are apt. They will be helpful none the less. The instance may be rejected, but the principle abides.

It is a rule of the common law that a surety is discharged from liability if the time of payment is extended by contract between the principal debtor and the creditor without the surety's consent. Even an extension for a single day will be sufficient to bring about that result.[11] Without such an extension, the surety would have the privilege upon the maturity of the debt of making payment to the creditor, and demanding immediate subrogation to the latter's remedies

[11] N. Y. Life Ins. Co. v. Casey, 178 N. Y. 381.

against the principal. He must, therefore, it is said, be deemed to have suffered prejudice if, by extension of the due date, the right has been postponed. I have no doubt that this rule may justly be applied whenever the surety can show that the extension has resulted in actual damage, as where the principal in the interval has become insolvent, or the value of the security has been impaired, though even in such circumstances the measure of exoneration ought in justice to be determined by the extent of the damage suffered. Perhaps there might be justice in permitting exoneration whenever the surety had tendered payment of the debt, and demanded subrogation to the remedies against the debtor. Perhaps the burden of disproving prejudice ought to be cast upon the creditor. No such limitations have been recognized. The rule applies to cases where neither tender nor actual damage is established or pretended. The law has shaped its judgments upon the fictitious assumption that a surety, who has probably lain awake at nights for fear that payment may some day be demanded, has in truth been smarting under the repressed desire to force an unwelcome payment on a reluctant or capricious creditor. The extended period has gone by; the surety has made no move, has not even troubled himself to inquire; yet he is held to be released on the theory that were it not for the extension, of which he knew nothing, and by which his conduct could not have been controlled, he would have come forward voluntarily with a tender of the debt. Such rules are survivals of the days when commercial dealings were simpler, when surety companies were unknown, when sureties were commonly generous friends whose confidence had been abused, and when the main effort of the courts seems to have been to find some plausible excuse for letting them out of their engagements. Already I see some signs of a change of spirit in decisions of recent dates.[12] I think we may well ask ourselves whether courts are not under a duty to go

[12] Wilkinson v. McKemmie, 229 U. S. 590, 593; U. S. v. McMullen, 222 U. S. 460, 468; Richardson v. County of Steuben, 226 N. Y. 13; Assets Realization Co. v. Roth, 226 N. Y. 370.

farther, and place this branch of the law upon a basis more consistent with the realities of business experience and the moralities of life.

It is another rule of the common law that a parol agreement, though subsequently made, is ineffective to vary or discharge a contract under seal.[13] In days when seals counted for a good deal, there may have been some reason in this recognition of a mystical solemnity. In our day, when the perfunctory initials "L. S." have replaced the heraldic devices, the law is conscious of its own absurdity when it preserves the rubrics of a vanished era.[14] Judges have made worthy, if shamefaced, efforts, while giving lip service to the rule, to riddle it with exceptions and by distinctions reduce it to a shadow.[15] A recent case suggests that timidity, and not reverence, has postponed the hour of dissolution.[16] The law

[13] McCreery v. Day, 119 N. Y. 1; 3 Williston on Contracts, secs. 1835, 1836.

[14] Harris v. Shorall, 230 N. Y. 343.

[15] McCreery v. Day, *supra;* Thomson v. Poor, 147 N. Y. 402.

[16] Harris v. Shorall, *supra.*

will have cause for gratitude to the deliverer who will strike the fatal blow.

I have drawn illustrations from the field of substantive law. The law of evidence and generally the whole subject of procedure supply fields where change may properly be made with a freedom even greater. The considerations of policy that dictate adherence to existing rules where substantive rights are involved, apply with diminished force when it is a question of the law of remedies. Let me take an illustration from the law of evidence. A man is prosecuted for rape. His defense is that the woman consented. He may show that her *reputation* for chastity is bad. He may not show specific, even though repeated, acts of unchastity with another man or other men.[17] The one thing that any sensible trier of the facts would wish to know above all others in estimating the truth of his defense is held by an inflexible rule to be something that must be excluded from the consideration of the jury. Even though the woman takes

[17] People v. Carey, 223 N. Y. 519.

the stand herself, the defendant is not greatly helped, for though he may then cross-examine her about other acts, he is concluded by her answer. Undoubtedly a judge should exercise a certain discretion in the admission of such evidence, should exclude it if too remote, and should be prompt by granting a continuance or otherwise to obviate any hardship resulting from surprise. That is not the effect of the present rule. The evidence is excluded altogether and always. Some courts, indeed, have taken a different view, but their number unfortunately is small. Here, as in many other branches of the law of evidence, we see an exaggerated reliance upon general reputation as a test for the ascertainment of the character of litigants or witnesses. Such a faith is a survival of more simple times. It was justified in days when men lived in small communities. Perhaps it has some justification even now in rural districts. In the life of great cities, it has made evidence of character a farce. Here, as in many other branches of adjective law, a spirit of realism should bring about a harmony between present rules and present needs.

None the less, the rule of adherence to precedent is applied with less rigidity in the United States than in England, and, I think, with a rigidity that is diminishing even here. The House of Lords holds itself absolutely bound by its own prior decisions.[18] The United States Supreme Court and the highest courts of the several states overrule their own prior decisions when manifestly erroneous.[19] Pollock, in a paper entitled "The Science of Case Law," written more than forty years ago, spoke of the freedom with which this was done, as suggesting that the law was nothing more than a matter of individual opinion.[20] Since then the tendency has, if anything, increased. An extreme illustration may be

[18] Gray, *supra*, sec. 462; Salmond, "Jurisprudence," p. 164, sec. 64; Pound, "Juristic Science and the Law," 31 Harvard L. R. 1053; London Street Tramways Co. v. London County Council, 1898, A. C. 375, 379.

[19] Pollock, "First Book of Jurisprudence," pp. 319, 320; Gray, "Judicial Precedents," 9 Harvard L. R. 27, 40.

[20] "Essays in Jurisprudence and Ethics," p. 245.

found in a recent decision of a federal court.[21] The plaintiff sued a manufacturer of automobiles to recover damages for personal injuries resulting from a defective car. On the first trial he had a verdict, which the Circuit Court of Appeals for the second circuit reversed on the ground that the manufacturer owed no duty to the plaintiff, the occupant of the car, since the latter was not the original purchaser, but had bought from some one else.[22] On a second trial, the judge, in obedience to this ruling, dismissed the complaint, and a writ of error brought the case before the same appellate court again. In the meantime, the New York Court of Appeals had held, in an action against another manufacturer, that there was a duty in such circumstances, irrespective of privity of contract.[23] The federal court followed that decision, overruled its prior ruling, and reversed the judgment of dismissal which had been entered in compliance with its mandate. The defendant in that case who first reversed the

[21] Johnson v. Cadillac Motor Co., 261 Fed. Rep. 878.
[22] 221 Fed. Rep. 801.
[23] MacPherson v. Buick Motor Co., 217 N. Y. 382.

judgment because the complaint had *not* been dismissed, and then suffered a reversal because on the same evidence the complaint *had* been dismissed, probably has some views of his own about the nature of the judicial process. I do not attempt to say whether departure from the rule of adherence to precedent was justified in such conditions. One judge dissenting held the view that the earlier decision should have been applied as the law of the case irrespective of its correctness, like the rules of *res adjudicata*. The conclusion of the majority of the court, whether right or wrong, is interesting as evidence of a spirit and a tendency to subordinate precedent to justice. How to reconcile that tendency, which is a growing and in the main a wholesome one, with the need of uniformity and certainty, is one of the great problems confronting the lawyers and judges of our day. We shall have to feel our way here as elsewhere in the law. Somewhere between worship of the past and exaltation of the present the path of safety will be found.

ADHERENCE TO PRECEDENT

Our survey of judicial methods teaches us, I think, the lesson that the whole subject matter of jurisprudence is more plastic, more malleable, the moulds less definitively cast, the bounds of right and wrong less preordained and constant, than most of us, without the aid of some such analysis, have been accustomed to believe. We like to picture to ourselves the field of the law as accurately mapped and plotted. We draw our little lines, and they are hardly down before we blur them. As in time and space, so here. Divisions are working hypotheses, adopted for convenience. We are tending more and more toward an appreciation of the truth that, after all, there are few rules; there are chiefly standards and degrees. It is a question of degree whether I have been negligent. It is a question of degree whether in the use of my own land, I have created a nuisance which may be abated by my neighbor. It is a question of degree whether the law which takes my property and limits my conduct impairs my liberty unduly. So also the duty of a judge becomes itself a question of degree, and he is a useful judge or a poor one as he estimates the measure accurately or loosely. He must balance all his ingredients, his philosophy, his logic, his analogies, his history, his customs, his sense of right, and all the rest, and adding a little here and taking out a little there, must determine, as wisely as he can, which weight shall tip the scales. If this seems a weak and inconclusive summary, I am not sure that the fault is mine. I know he is a wise pharmacist who from a recipe so general can compound a fitting remedy. But the like criticism may be made of most attempts to formulate the principles which regulate the practice of an art. W. Jethro Brown reminds us in a recent paper on "Law and Evolution"[24] that "Sir Joshua Reynolds' book on painting, offers little or no guidance to those who wish to become famous painters. Books on literary styles are notoriously lacking, speaking as a rule, in practical utility." After the wearisome process of analysis has been finished, there must be for every judge a new synthesis which

[24] 29 Yale L. J. 394, 397.

he will have to make for himself. The most that he can hope for is that with long thought and study, with years of practice at the bar or on the bench, and with the aid of that inward grace which comes now and again to the elect of any calling, the analysis may help a little to make the synthesis a true one.

In what I have said, I have thrown, perhaps too much, into the background and the shadow the cases where the controversy turns not upon the rule of law, but upon its application to the facts. Those cases, after all, make up the bulk of the business of the courts. They are important for the litigants concerned in them. They call for intelligence and patience and reasonable discernment on the part of the judges who must decide them. But they leave jurisprudence where it stood before. As applied to such cases, the judicial process, as was said at the outset of these lectures, is a process of search and comparison, and little else. We have to distinguish between the precedents which are merely static, and those

which are dynamic.[25] Because the former out-
number the latter many times, a sketch of the
judicial process which concerns itself almost
exclusively with the creative or dynamic element, is likely to give a false impression, an
overcolored picture, of uncertainty in the law and
of free discretion in the judge. Of the cases that
come before the court in which I sit, a majority,
I think, could not, with semblance of reason, be
decided in any way but one. The law and its
application alike are plain. Such cases are pre-
destined, so to speak, to affirmance without
opinion. In another and considerable percentage,
the rule of law is certain, and the application
alone doubtful. A complicated record must be
dissected, the narratives of witnesses, more or
less incoherent and unintelligible, must be
analyzed, to determine whether a given situation
comes within one district or another upon the
chart of rights and wrongs. The traveler who
knows that a railroad crosses his path must look
for approaching trains. That is at least the gen-

[25] Cf. Salmond, "Jurisprudence," p. 160.

eral rule. In numberless litigations the description of the landscape must be studied to see whether vision has been obstructed, whether something has been done or omitted to put the traveler off his guard. Often these cases and others like them provoke difference of opinion among judges. Jurisprudence remains untouched, however, regardless of the outcome. Finally there remains a percentage, not large indeed, and yet not so small as to be negligible, where a decision one way or the other, will count for the future, will advance or retard, sometimes much, sometimes little, the development of the law. These are the cases where the creative element in the judicial process finds its opportunity and power. It is with these cases that I have chiefly concerned myself in all that I have said to you. In a sense it is true of many of them that they might be decided either way. By that I mean that reasons plausible and fairly persuasive might be found for one conclusion as for another. Here come into play that balancing of judgment, that testing and sorting of considerations of analogy and logic and utility and fairness, which I have been trying to describe. Here it is that the judge assumes the function of a lawgiver. I was much troubled in spirit, in my first years upon the bench, to find how trackless was the ocean on which I had embarked. I sought for certainty. I was oppressed and disheartened when I found that the quest for it was futile. I was trying to reach land, the solid land of fixed and settled rules, the paradise of a justice that would declare itself by tokens plainer and more commanding than its pale and glimmering reflections in my own vacillating mind and conscience. I found "with the voyagers in Browning's 'Paracelsus' that the real heaven was always beyond."[26] As the years have gone by, and as I have reflected more and more upon the nature of the judicial process, I have become reconciled to the uncertainty, because I have grown to see it as inevitable. I have grown to see that the process in its highest reaches is not discovery, but creation;

[26] G. Lowes Dickinson, "Religion and Immortality," p. 70.

and that the doubts and misgivings, the hopes and fears, are part of the travail of mind, the pangs of death and the pangs of birth, in which principles that have served their day expire, and new principles are born.

I have spoken of the forces of which judges avowedly avail to shape the form and content of their judgments. Even these forces are seldom fully in consciousness. They lie so near the surface, however, that their existence and influence are not likely to be disclaimed. But the subject is not exhausted with the recognition of their power. Deep below consciousness are other forces, the likes and the dislikes, the predilections and the prejudices, the complex of instincts and emotions and habits and convictions, which make the man, whether he be litigant or judge. I wish I might have found the time and opportunity to pursue this subject farther. I shall be able, as it is, to do little more than remind you of its existence.[27] There has been a certain lack of

[27] An interesting study of this subject will be found in a book published since these lectures were written,

candor in much of the discussion of the theme, or rather perhaps in the refusal to discuss it, as if judges must lose respect and confidence by the reminder that they are subject to human limitations. I do not doubt the grandeur of the conception which lifts them into the realm of pure reason, above and beyond the sweep of perturbing and deflecting forces. None the less, if there is anything of reality in my analysis of the judicial process, they do not stand aloof on these chill and distant heights; and we shall not help the cause of truth by acting and speaking as if they do. The great tides and currents which engulf the rest of men do not turn aside in their course and pass the judges by. We like to figure to ourselves the processes of justice as coldly objective and impersonal. The law, conceived of as a real existence, dwelling apart and alone, speaks, through the voices of priests and ministers, the words which they have no choice except to utter. That is an ideal of objective truth toward which

"The Foundations of Social Science," by James Mickel Williams, p. 209 *et seq.*

every system of jurisprudence tends. It is an ideal of which great publicists and judges have spoken as of something possible to attain. "The judges of the nation," says Montesquieu, "are only the mouths that pronounce the words of the law, inanimate beings, who can moderate neither its force nor its rigor."[28] So Marshall, in Osborne v. Bank of the United States, 9 Wheat. 738, 866: The judicial department "has no will in any case. . . . Judicial power is never exercised for the purpose of giving effect to the will of the judge; always for the purpose of giving effect to the will of the legislature; or in other words, to the will of the law." It has a lofty sound; it is well and finely said; but it can never be more than partly true. Marshall's own career is a conspicuous illustration of the fact that the ideal is beyond the reach of human faculties to attain. He gave to the constitution of the United States the impress of his own mind; and the form of

[28] Montesquieu, "Esprit des Lois," LIV, XI, chap. VI, quoted by Ehrlich, "Die juristische Logik," p. 101; Gény, op. cit., p. 76; cf. Flavius, supra, p. 40.

our constitutional law is what it is, because he
moulded it while it was still plastic and malleable in the fire of his own intense convictions.
At the opposite extreme are the words of the
French jurist, Saleilles, in his treatise "De la
Personnalité Juridique":[29] "One wills at the beginning the result; one finds the principle after-
wards; such is the genesis of all juridical construction. Once accepted, the construction pre-
sents itself, doubtless, in the ensemble of legal
doctrine, under the opposite aspect. The factors
are inverted. The principle appears as an initial
cause, from which one has drawn the result
which is found deduced from it." I would not
put the case thus broadly. So sweeping a statement exaggerates the element of free volition. It
ignores the factors of determinism which cabin
and confine within narrow bounds the range
of unfettered choice. None the less, by its very
excess of emphasis, it supplies the needed cor-
rective of an ideal of impossible objectivity.
Nearer to the truth, and midway between these

[29] Pp. 45, 46.

extremes, are the words of a man who was not a jurist, but whose intuitions and perceptions were deep and brilliant—the words of President Roosevelt in his message of December 8, 1908, to the Congress of the United States:[30] "The chief lawmakers in our country may be, and often are, the judges, because they are the final seat of authority. Every time they interpret contract, property, vested rights, due process of law, liberty, they necessarily enact into law parts of a system of social philosophy; and as such interpretation is fundamental, they give direction to all law-making. The decisions of the courts on economic and social questions depend upon their economic and social philosophy; and for the peaceful progress of our people during the twentieth century we shall owe most to those judges who hold to a twentieth century economic and social philosophy and not to a long outgrown philosophy, which was itself the product of primitive economic conditions."

I remember that this statement when made

[30] 43 Congressional Record, part 1, p. 21.

aroused a storm of criticism. It betrayed ignorance, they said, of the nature of the judicial
process. The business of the judge, they told us,
was to discover objective truth. His own little
individuality, his tiny stock of scattered and
unco-ordinated philosophies, these, with all his
weaknesses and unconscious prejudices, were to
be laid aside and forgotten. What did men care
for *his* reading of the eternal verities? It was
not worth recording. What the world was seeking was the eternal verities themselves. Far am
I from denying that this is, indeed, the goal
toward which all of us must strive. Something of
Pascal's spirit of self-search and self-reproach
must come at moments to the man who finds
himself summoned to the duty of shaping the
progress of the law. The very breadth and scope
of the opportunity to give expression to his
finer self seem to point the accusing finger of
disparagement and scorn. What am I that in
these great movements onward, this rush and
sweep of forces, my petty personality should de-
flect them by a hairbreadth? Why should the

pure light of truth be broken up and impregnated and colored with any element of my being? Such doubts and hesitations besiege one now and again. The truth is, however, that all these inward questionings are born of the hope and desire to transcend the limitations which hedge our human nature. Roosevelt, who knew men, had no illusions on this score. He was not positing an ideal. He was not fixing a goal. He was measuring the powers and the endurance of those by whom the race was to be run. My duty as judge may be to objectify in law, not my own aspirations and convictions and philosophies, but the aspirations and convictions and philosophies of the men and women of my time. Hardly shall I do this well if my own sympathies and beliefs and passionate devotions are with a time that is past. "We shall never be able to flatter ourselves, in any system of judicial interpretation, that we have eliminated altogether the personal measure of the interpreter. In the moral sciences, there is no method or procedure which entirely supplants subjective reason."[31] We may figure the task of the judge, if we please, as the task of a translator, the reading of signs and symbols given from without. None the less, we will not set men to such a task, unless they have absorbed the spirit, and have filled themselves with a love, of the language they must read.

I have no quarrel, therefore, with the doctrine that judges ought to be in sympathy with the spirit of their times. Alas! assent to such a generality does not carry us far upon the road to truth. In every court there are likely to be as many estimates of the "Zeitgeist" as there are judges on its bench. Of the power of favor or prejudice in any sordid or vulgar or evil sense, I have found no trace, not even the faintest, among the judges whom I have known. But every day there is borne in on me a new conviction of the inescapable relation between the truth without us and the truth within. The spirit of the age, as it is revealed to each of us, is too often only

[31] Gény, *op. cit.*, vol. II, p. 93, sec. 159; vol. II, p. 142, sec. 168; also Flavius, p. 43.

the spirit of the group in which the accidents of birth or education or occupation or fellowship have given us a place. No effort or revolution of the mind will overthrow utterly and at all times the empire of these subconscious loyalties. "Our beliefs and opinions," says James Harvey Robinson,[32] "like our standards of conduct come to us insensibly as products of our companionship with our fellow men, not as results of our personal experience and the inferences we individually make from our own observations. We are constantly misled by our extraordinary faculty of 'rationalizing'—that is, of devising plausible arguments for accepting what is imposed upon us by the traditions of the group to which we belong. We are abjectly credulous by nature, and instinctively accept the verdicts of the group. We are suggestible not merely when under the spell of an excited mob or a fervent revival, but we are ever and always listening to the still small voice of the herd, and are ever ready to defend and

[32] "The Still Small Voice of the Herd," 32 Political Science Quarterly 315.

justify its instructions and warnings, and accept them as the mature results of our own reasoning." This was written, not of judges specially, but of men and women of all classes. The training of the judge, if coupled with what is styled the judicial temperament, will help in some degree to emancipate him from the suggestive power of individual dislikes and prepossessions. It will help to broaden the group to which his subconscious loyalties are due. Never will these loyalties be utterly extinguished while human nature is what it is. We may wonder sometimes how from the play of all these forces of individualism, there can come anything coherent, anything but chaos and the void. Those are the moments in which we exaggerate the elements of difference. In the end there emerges something which has a composite shape and truth and order. It has been said that "History, like mathematics, is obliged to assume that eccentricities more or less balance each other, so that something remains constant at last."[33] The like is true of the

[33] Henry Adams, "The Degradation of the Democratic Dogma," pp. 291, 292.

work of courts. The eccentricities of judges balance one another. One judge looks at problems from the point of view of history, another from that of philosophy, another from that of social utility, one is a formalist, another a latitudinarian, one is timorous of change, another dissatisfied with the present; out of the attrition of diverse minds there is beaten something which has a constancy and uniformity and average value greater than its component elements. The same thing is true of the work of juries. I do not mean to suggest that the product in either case does not betray the flaws inherent in its origin. The flaws are there as in every human institution. Because they are not only there but visible, we have faith that they will be corrected. There is no assurance that the rule of the majority will be the expression of perfect reason when embodied in constitution or in statute. We ought not to expect more of it when embodied in the judgments of the courts. The tide rises and falls, but the sands of error crumble.

CONCLUSION

The work of a judge is in one sense enduring and in another sense ephemeral. What is good in it endures. What is erroneous is pretty sure to perish. The good remains the foundation on which new structures will be built. The bad will be rejected and cast off in the laboratory of the years. Little by little the old doctrine is undermined. Often the encroachments are so gradual that their significance is at first obscured. Finally we discover that the contour of the landscape has been changed, that the old maps must be cast aside, and the ground charted anew. The process, with all its silent yet inevitable power, has been described by Mr. Henderson with singular felicity:[34] "When an adherent of a systematic faith is brought continuously in touch with influences and exposed to desires inconsistent with that faith, a process of unconscious cerebration may take place, by which a growing store of hostile mental inclinations may accumulate,

[34] "Foreign Corporations in American Constitutional Law," p. 164; cf. Powell, "The Changing Law of Foreign Corporations," 33 Pol. Science Quarterly, p. 569.

strongly motivating action and decision, but seldom emerging clearly into consciousness. In the meantime the formulas of the old faith are retained and repeated by force of habit, until one day the realization comes that conduct and sympathies and fundamental desires have become so inconsistent with the logical framework that it must be discarded. Then begins the task of building up and rationalizing a new faith."

Ever in the making, as law develops through the centuries, is this new faith which silently and steadily effaces our mistakes and eccentricities. I sometimes think that we worry ourselves overmuch about the enduring consequences of our errors. They may work a little confusion for a time. In the end, they will be modified or corrected or their teachings ignored. The future takes care of such things. In the endless process of testing and retesting, there is a constant rejection of the dross, and a constant retention of whatever is pure and sound and fine.

The future, gentlemen, is yours. We have been called to do our parts in an ageless process. Long

CONCLUSION

after I am dead and gone, and my little part in it is forgotten, you will be here to do your share, and to carry the torch forward. I know that the flame will burn bright while the torch is in your keeping.